"Lisa is funny and refreshingly honest about herself and her yeses. She treats other people's stories of difficult yeses with the reverence and dignity they deserve. I laughed and cried and saw myself many times over in this book."

Deanna Bartalini
The New Evangelizers

"In an age where we are called to be active participants in the new evangelization, we need to focus a bit on ourselves as well. With Lisa's guidance and example, at the end of this book you will find it a little easier to say yes in your own way."

Pete Socks
The Catholic Book Blogger

"Lisa Hendey has much wisdom to offer on all of these virtues, and one can only appreciate her honesty and willingness to share the messiness of her own life in order to encourage others. *The Grace of Yes* is an excellent book that will give you much to ponder."

Patrice Fagnant-MacArthur
Catholic Lane

"Lisa Hendey has created an incredibly readable introspection into the many yeses in life that make up our journey to a life of faith."

Allison Gingras
Reconciled to You

"*The Grace of Yes* is a wonderful mix of stardust and Crisco—a blending of the mystical with getting dinner on the table. There is a lot in this little book: a lot of big things, a lot of surprises, and a lot of truth. There is an honesty that's hard to find these days. And I think there is a prescription for exactly what we need in these days: to say 'yes' to God."

Jake Frost
Catholic Lane

"We spend so much time thinking about the yeses in our calendars, our checkbooks, our parenting and other relationships that we sometimes forget the most important yes of all—our response to the call of God. Hendey shares her wisdom, her heart, and her experiences to remind us and refine us as we read. I give this book a resounding YES!"

Kristin Armstrong
Author of *Happily Ever After*

"*The Grace of Yes* is classic Lisa Hendey. Lisa's transparency and candor, coupled with her experiences of living a life fully engaged, make this book well worth reading and sharing. Anyone seeking a path to more virtuous Catholic living should buy this excellent book!"

Randy Hain
Author of *The Journey to Heaven*

"*The Grace of Yes* shows why Lisa Hendey resonates with so many people around the world. With clear, accessible language, she teaches that the profound lessons of the Gospel can inform our daily lives. Every one of our interactions and every one of our decisions give us the opportunity to learn and grow in the way God intended. Lisa understands that, and when you read this book, you will, too."

Carolyn Y. Woo
Former president and CEO of Catholic Relief Services

"'No' is safe. 'No' is simple. But 'no' isn't always the right answer. Lisa Hendey's *The Grace of Yes* teaches, challenges, and encourages us how to say yes to God and others. Should you read this book? Yes! And God's grace will work within you."

Lino Rulli
Host of *The Catholic Guy*

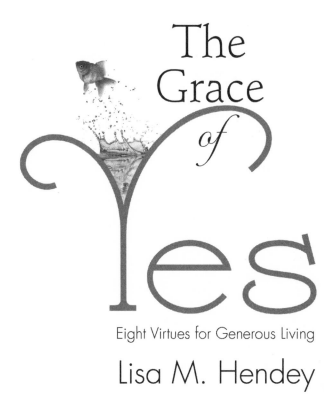

The Grace *of* Yes

Eight Virtues for Generous Living

Lisa M. Hendey

AVE MARIA PRESS AVE Notre Dame, Indiana

Founded in 1865, Ave Maria Press is a ministry of the United States Province of Holy Cross.

www.avemariapress.com

Paperback: ISBN-13 978-1-59471-472-6

E-book: ISBN-13 978-1-59471-473-3

Cover image © Thinkstockphotos.com

Cover and text design by Katherine Robinson.

Printed and bound in the United States of America.

Library of Congress Cataloging-in-Publication Data

Hendey, Lisa M.

   The grace of yes : eight virtues for generous living / Lisa M. Hendey.

      pages cm

   Includes bibliographical references.

   ISBN 978-1-59471-472-6

   1. Christian life--Catholic authors. I. Title.

   BX2350.3.H46 2014

   248.4'82--dc23

                        2014019624

To Greg,
thank you for a lifetime of yes.

Contents

Preface

My parents believed, and I trusted them. So I believed. We believed in God and salvation through Jesus Christ, and we lived our beliefs as Roman Catholics. Ask me exactly what I believed growing up and what I believe today and the Catholic-school-educated, Mass-going, doctrine-quoting me will recite the tenets of the Nicene Creed—a profession of the faith into which I was baptized as an infant, in a Church I've loved with a blinding passion all my life. Ask me if I have ever doubted, questioned, or even knowingly rejected my creed, and if I'm being honest, I will with tender remorse answer yes. I am, of course, a sinner—but a hopeful, optimistic one. I trust that grace will save me.

I'm fairly certain that at the heart of every Christian believer is a determined will to not only share the Good News but also to radiate at least a small glimmer of God's love to everyone we meet. At the core of each of us lies the conviction that by encountering us, others ought to know at least some tiny measure of God's enduring love. Because I believe this, I have tried to submit my life to God, the source of every good gift. I want to live my life loving God by generously giving the best

parts of what he has created in me to the service and
love of others.

The more I ponder the connection between my faith
and all the other pieces of my life, the more intimately I
am able to see the unbroken bond between God's infinite
grace and my profound desire to consistently choose the
path of greatest generosity. I don't make this statement
boastfully. As a wife, a mother, a writer, and a Christian
trudging a daily footpath toward Christ, I am ever cognizant of my shortcomings. But I've also been at this
journey long enough to recognize God's fascinating and
loving hand at work in my life, especially in moments
where grace—God's deep, abiding blessing—is the only
plausible explanation for the goodness that's been showered on me.

I am reminded of the opening verses of the Letter to the Hebrews, which in my Catholic Bible reads,
"Faith is the realization of what is hoped for and evidence of things not seen" (11:1). In my fifty-plus years of
walking with Christ, I have repeatedly found surprising
and intriguing evidence of things not seen. Faith is the
connection—the spiritual bridge—between the lingering doubts I sometimes have and the discipline of "Yes,
Lord, I believe."

As I grow along my path as a Christian, I want to
more radically commit myself to generosity of spirit—a
gift of the stuff that God has placed within me to the
work he puts before me. Generous living doesn't simply
mean to be a financial giver or the person who can be
relied upon to help out in a pinch. Rather, I'm learning
that generous living is a consistent, gentle stoking of

the embers placed within us into blazing fires of action, mission, transformative change, and loving service. I believe that when you and I err on the side of giving our own unique yeses to the call of God, we have the capacity to rock our world.

My hope for the exploration of the eight virtues around which this book is built is that you claim anew the faith-inspired yeses of your own life. I hope you share my delight and fascination with God's loving hand at work in our lives. But let's allow our marveling to be only the first step in a long process. A true yes to God means moving from profound recognition and delight to lasting, steady commitment, even when we doubt, fear, or simply feel exhausted.

Generous living entails both openness to God's plan and a plan of our own. We each need a plan for total engagement in the virtues that lie at the heart of generous living: belief, generativity, creativity, integrity, humility, vulnerability, saying no, and rebirth. I hope that recognizing and seizing the grace of yes in your life will be a gift for you, as it has been for me, and will help you get started—for the first time or once again—on the sacred path of generosity.

I encourage you to ponder the questions at the end of each chapter on your own or with trusted friends. The prayers that close each chapter are my words, placed there to invite you into dialogue with our loving Creator. May this book help to crystalize in your mind and heart the gifts of your own unique yes, your own path of generous giving along life's path to heaven. I share with you some of my story and invite you to connect it to your own. Together may we praise God, who pokes, prods, and kindly leads us toward the awesome grace of ever-deepening yes.

1. The Grace *of* Belief

My mom, an only child, went off to Mass every Sunday with her mother, Bessie, while her father, Leroy, a deacon in the Lutheran church down the street from their Catholic one, said his own yes with a Missouri Synod accent. Two parents, two Christian denominations, one daughter, and a singular love for the Lord—it all worked beautifully for them.

My dad, the eldest of seven, was a mischievous altar boy raised by daily communicants in the Catholic Church. His parents, Wayne and Patty, reared seven spiritual seekers who ultimately chose diverse, and at times unconventional, spiritual paths but always respected their parents' unending commitment to their beliefs. Growing up, we were told that Grandma Patty's extended family was distantly connected to St. Thérèse of Lisieux, the Little Flower. When I picture some of my favorite female saints, they physically resemble Grandma Patty. And in my mind's eye Grandpa Wayne stands beside these holy women, unwavering in his beliefs, his faith solid as a rock.

I came along as a surprise in 1963, born only ten months after my parents' big Catholic wedding and the firstborn grandchild on both sides of the family. My childhood was a continual object lesson in remaining open to God's plan. The eldest of five, I grew up in a home that epitomized "domestic church" before that phrase came into the popular Catholic lexicon. Don't get me wrong; ours wasn't an overly reverent or somber upbringing. I was catechized in the 1970s, when folk Masses were the rage and our school nuns rode skateboards.

I may not have been brought up on the Baltimore Catechism, but I knew beyond a shadow of a doubt that Jesus loved me. That sense of ultimate security was owed in near totality to my parents and to Msgr. Michael Collins, the Irish priest who was our pastor for many years. Truly believing that I was loved unconditionally and favored beyond measure was a blessing, but it also came with a mandate. Our gifts—spiritual, relational, and material—were destined to be shared with those around us. Faith came with duty. And it came with great joy.

I always believed. My faith life grew as a gift from my parents, who had inherited their faiths and practices from theirs. My childhood faith was simple, unquestioning. I sat at the feet of the Christ I saw depicted in my picture bible, anxious like those little children in Matthew's nineteenth chapter, gathering close to receive his blessing. Jesus loved me. I was sure of it.

When I received Confirmation in eighth grade, my religion teacher taught me that by merit of this third Catholic sacrament I was called to be a witness to the faith in word and in deed. I was more perfectly bound by it to the Church and strengthened by the gifts of the Holy Spirit. I have to admit that I was far more concerned with the dress I was wearing that day and with how my hair looked than about how I would witness to others.

But the strength of the Spirit began to labor within the groundwork that had been laid so firmly by my parents. Slowly, imperceptibly, the trust that I had always had in them and what they had taught me became my own belief not only in a loving, all-powerful God but also in his Church. By the time I landed for my freshman year at the University of Notre Dame, I was fully committed to my beliefs and to offering a strong witness of them by my practice of Catholicism.

It was easy—and, honestly, fun—to be a believer at Notre Dame in the early 1980s. Mass was prayed in the company of our dormitory friends every night of the week. I often lingered in prayer at the campus grotto, lighting a candle as I offered my prayers, confident that God would hear and answer my needs. I became a daily communicant and saw signs of vibrant faith transformed into service all around me on campus. Having been raised so solidly Catholic and seeing my interior faith life blossom, I embraced my belief in God and in the Catholic Church with little to no doubt. My prayer life flourished, my devotion to the Blessed Mother grew, and my enthusiasm for Christian service deepened. I loved being Catholic.

I can see now that believing back then was largely a "What's in it for me?" proposal. I believed that God would hear and answer my prayers. I did not yet understand the mandate that being a believer also meant being first and foremost a generous spirit.

Wings

It wasn't until after my college graduation that I stopped equating going to church with having fun. While I had a few Protestant friends growing up—and was at one time a card-carrying member of the Good News Club (albeit horrible at memorizing scripture verses)—I rarely had encountered anyone who didn't share my Catholic beliefs. So when my engagement to Greg Hendey whisked me out of graduate school in Phoenix, Arizona, and into the life of a working girl in the Bible-belt city of Nashville, Tennessee, my spiritual frame of reference was flipped on its head. I found myself working full time in an office full of Southern Baptists who considered my religious pedigree questionable at best. One friend in my office, a faith-filled young woman, actually told me that for her to have married a Roman Catholic would have been more devastating to her parents than had she "hooked up with a Hare Krishna."

Greg, a fellow graduate of Notre Dame, had been nominally raised Lutheran but really wasn't a religious person. He had been thrust into a fully Catholic world at Notre Dame, and while he'd gone with the flow, he didn't have strong feelings on the topic—or at least he didn't express them at the time. I recall a heart-to-heart conversation with my father as things were getting serious with Greg. I had assured Daddy that Greg was a good person and that we had agreed to raise our children in the Catholic faith. I can see now that I had no concept of what that really meant or just how challenging it would prove to be.

Nashville brought my first real encounter with spiritual doubt. Greg was swamped with his studies as a first-year medical student, which meant that I often went to church alone. This was a lifetime first, and going to church became a struggle. After a lifetime of worshipping with family and friends, the expression of my faith became a solitary pursuit. The seeds that had been sown so lovingly by my parents and that had blossomed so well at Notre Dame began to wither and fade. I didn't stop believing. It just began to feel like work. Perhaps, for the very first time, my yes was my own. And I gave it begrudgingly.

As a part of our wedding vows, Greg and I promised to raise our children Catholic. In actuality, that promise was all on me, since I was the Catholic in the relationship. Greg couldn't have been more awesome about going along with our commitment and my wishes. In the early years of our marriage, before our children were born, he helped me find various churches as our life together took us through medical school in Nashville and on to his residency at UCLA. Greg would come with me to church as often as his schedule permitted, but it often didn't. It was in those first five years together that I came to more fully understand the words "Sunday obligation." Even though Sunday-morning Mass had been the focal point of my life for so many years, I'm sad to say that I often sat in the pew alone, feeling unfulfilled. All too often, I left not only uninspired but also frustrated and grumbling to myself, "I didn't get anything out of that."

The fifty-year-old Lisa would love to go back in time to that twenty-something yuppie and talk some sense into her. Somehow, even though I had lived a quarter-century learning scripture and Church teachings, two important concepts were missing from my frame of reference. First and foremost, I didn't really grasp the centrality of the Eucharist as a core *belief* in my faith, although attending Mass had always been a core practice. Second, and equally as disappointing to me now, was a lack of awareness of my responsibility to be an active part of my faith community, to put something *in* rather than just get something *out* of worship.

During our early marriage, I tried out many pews, church-shopping my way around Southern California and looking for a pastor who was entertaining in a church that was pretty and had good music. I see now that my search was for the wrong things. I was a consumer, not a giver or a true member of the Body of Christ. I was like a family member who showed up looking for a place to stay but refusing to commit in any way to building a bond. I was not yet mature enough in my beliefs to recognize that as a Christian, my church was a second family that had the same core need for my self-giving as my own nuclear family did.

The perfect-church characteristics I shopped for and thought I needed were most neatly delivered in a small parish in Seal Beach, California, where my parents had moved when Greg and I were getting settled in Los Angeles. By strange coincidence or divine intervention, I was reunited with my childhood pastor, Msgr. Collins, behind the altar at that church. He was now aging but still full of humor and an infectious faith. In that tidy little seaside church, his lilting Irish accent proclaimed the gospel reading in a way that began to beckon me back to long-forgotten truths. When we brought our firstborn, Eric Michael (named in honor of that holy man), forward for Baptism in that little Seal Beach slice of heaven, Greg and I stood together at the baptismal font, renewed our Baptismal promises to live as faithful Christians, and committed to raise Eric in that same faith and way of life.

It was at that moment that the words to an old song I played on my guitar at church in my youth became marching orders for me.

> It only takes a spark, to get a fire going.
> And soon all those around, can warm up in its glowing.
> That's how it is with God's love, once you've experienced it,
> It's fresh like spring, you want to sing, you want to pass it on!

By that point my belief—my yes to those things I had been taught over so many years—was finally fully my own. I knew God's love. I had witnessed it so fully that I couldn't wait to share it with this precious little soul. Here was overwhelming evidence of grace.

We celebrated Eric's Baptism in my parents' home with a cake that proclaimed in bright blue icing: "Eric Michael, Child of God." I reasoned to myself that if Eric was God's child, I was Lisa Marie, Child of God's Mom. If Eric was to know and to love God, the job to help him do so was all mine. Surely Greg was a partner in that duty, but since he was not at that time formally affiliated with a church, I sensed the burden of rearing my child in the faith, of planting in him the seeds for his very own belief in God, and all that this would mean for Eric's life. That job expanded three years later when our second son, Adam Patrick, was born.

Passing It On

Our family's path toward belief played out over the next few years as we found a church home and settled in. Greg's career had settled us in Fresno, California, a beautiful city that seemed to have a church on every corner. Anxious to give our boys a Catholic education, we settled at the parish with what I perceived to be the best school in town.

Early in our time there, a playgroup friend who was converting to the faith asked me to be her sponsor as she prepared to enter the Catholic Church through the Rite of Christian Initiation of Adults (RCIA). Committing to serving as a sponsor meant journeying with April by attending her formation meetings and classes, being a spiritual companion, and praying for her as she studied the faith. When I gladly agreed, I thought I was doing my friend a favor. How easy it is to look back now and see that the opposite was actually true. In standing with

April and helping her to learn about her own beliefs, I was called to renew my own "Yes, Lord, I believe."

Helping April prepare to enter the Church also taught me a critical lesson about feeling at home with a parish: I needed to become an active part of the faith family I was joining. It wasn't enough to show up on Sunday and expect to walk away feeling fed. There had to be giving from my side, both to my new faith home and to my private prayer life.

This was also about the time that I began to measure my personal worthiness as a believer by the lives of those closest to me: Greg and my two little sons. Suddenly, more than ever, the disparity of religious practice between Greg and me began to gnaw at my spirit. I felt increasing pressure to pass along my love for God to our sons. If I didn't do this right, would they reject those things I held most dear in my life?

Into these shifting winds of my spiritual life, God sent Martha. She was a ministry leader in our parish whose eldest son was in Eric's kindergarten class. I had begun my friendship with Martha during April's journey into the Church. I wish I could recall the exact moment when we met, for it was clearly ordained by a God who knew that I would need a strong spiritual guide and companion for the journey that lay ahead of me. Over the years, Martha has been a trusted friend, a mentor who challenged me, and a shining example of the type of woman I desire to be. Everyone should have a Martha in his or her life—a partner who takes your hand and with no judgment leads you toward all that is true, just, and right, guiding you without dragging you.

Martha, my boys, and an all-loving God were a few of the key ingredients that helped Greg, my very best friend, find the perfect recipe for his own beliefs. At the Easter Vigil the year that our Adam was in second grade preparing for the sacraments of Reconciliation and Eucharist, the boys and I sat in the pews as Greg was sacramentally received into the Catholic Church. This moment that I had prayed and hoped so desperately for over the course of seventeen years happened in God's perfect time, not mine.

All along I had prayed for Greg's conversion when what I should really have been begging God for was my own. In witnessing my husband's profession of his beliefs and the way it played out in his personal journey, I had a glimpse of the joy God must feel when one of us turns toward him with an open heart and how much elation God must feel when the arms that have been reaching out to hold us close finally welcome us home into his loving embrace.

Greg's strong, solid witness to his beliefs is often more subtle than my approach. This has served as a reminder to me of those biblical teachings that under-score each individual's unique spiritual gifts. We read in the twelfth chapter of First Corinthians about the unity and variety of these gifts:

> There are different kinds of spiritual gifts but the same Spirit; there are different forms of service but the same Lord; there are different workings but the same God who produces all of them in everyone. To each individual

> the manifestation of the Spirit is given for
> some benefit. . . . But one and the same Spirit
> produces all of these, distributing them indi-
> vidually to each person as he wishes (1 Cor
> 12:4–7, 11).

Paul underscored the varied nature of the charisms the Corinthian community witnessed and taught these early Christians about the connection between the gifts and their source. The gifts were freely given by God out of an abundance of grace; they were destined to be used for the service of others; and the gifts were works of God, their Creator. Just as those early Christians learned that they each had a role to play in leading others into belief, I learned by watching Greg's walk of faith that we also complemented one another's gifts in our own home and in our parish community.

Journeying toward a common spiritual goal with my spouse has also taught me to judge neither our family's domestic church nor my own holiness by any-one else's measure. So often we blame or congratulate ourselves for the faith choices made by others. Our spouse converts and we beam with pride. Our chil-dren stray and we ask what we could have done to pre-vent it. Don't get me wrong here. I am not saying that we shouldn't pray with and for our loved ones. Our homes—our domestic churches—should be places of communal prayer and shared service. I'm simply say-ing that I have realized that my family is best served spiritually when I concern myself less with how holy my husband and sons are and worry more about my own personal relationship with the God who loves me perfectly despite my imperfection.

Can You Google God?

Let's fast-forward this story by a few years, past the noisy pew filled with screaming preschoolers and the "I don't want to go to church, Mommy!" moments to little Adam's early years in school. Something prompted me to take my quest to be a good Catholic mom to the web. I went looking for answers, and when I didn't find them online, I bought a domain name and some of those *For Dummies* books about the Internet and launched CatholicMom.com.

The site wasn't intended to give advice. Even back then our little corner of the World Wide Web was only what I still hope that it will always be: a means of discussing concepts of faith and journeying in love toward God with other spiritual seekers. What began as a hobby has become a daily mission that has not only strengthened my own knowledge of my faith but also has afforded me the chance to witness it in ways I never dreamed possible.

As I write this book, I still ask myself daily, "Are you sure, Lord? Is it I, Lord?" He could have chosen someone so much better equipped for the task of leading a website that combines the efforts of more than one hundred writers who share their gifts on a daily basis with readers in more than 140 countries around the world. What started as my hobby has become a shining light, a testament to the beauty of a solid life of belief. And I say this not to boast but truly to marvel at God's goodness and at the generosity of so many talented writers who are the heart and soul of the site. When you come now to visit our little corner of the web, you may not even know that it had its beginnings in my living room. And I consider that a success—that it's not "Lisa's site" but that it really belongs to the community of believers who meet there every day. From the platform of the website, I have written books, spoken on countless stages about faith and family topics, developed an expertise (of sorts) in the use of social media in the New Evangelization, and traveled the globe on faith and service missions.

And yet, there is still a daily "Yes, Lord" to the underlying call to use *these* tools in *this* way to lead others closer to God. In my morning prayers each day, I take a moment of quiet time to hear God's divine will for my life. At times, I envy those visionaries we read about who claim to have had an auditory or visual interaction with God—how profoundly amazing it must be to have the assurance that you're on the right track. I'll admit that I often beg him in my prayers for clarity of purpose, for some sign that the way I fill my days is at once pleasing and right according to his plan and not simply my own agenda. The more I work in the mission field, whether online, in churches, or with faith-based groups, the more my mantra becomes, "Your plan, my yes."

When you spend your waking hours working in the spiritual realm, there are very real dangers. One major one for me is to get caught up in all the hype about myself. Folks sometimes assume a holiness that often isn't merited. It's easy to have my head turned by book reviews or the number of "likes" my latest post had on

Facebook. Pride, especially spiritual pride, is a constant trap. The only way to avoid falling in is to know of the trap's existence, to shine a huge light in front of myself in hopes of seeing and avoiding it, and to cling to a huge dose of humble prayer.

In whatever realm you live out your spiritual calling, if you let the traps that stand in your way paralyze you from moving forward, you give in to the evil one who set those snares. If you foolishly consider that you will never be snared, you're a sitting duck. It's best to journey forward, cognizant of the risks but also humble and surrounded by spiritual companions who can haul you out of the pit when you occasionally lose your way and fall in. A generous believer gives others the gift of letting them help her—at least on occasion.

Giving It All to Him

The greatest danger I face in my work was eloquently spoken to me very recently by a priest I met. He is a well-known biblical scholar and the CEO of a major religious broadcasting corporation. When I asked how he balances his corporate and ministry duties with a strong prayer life—how he manages to do it all—he gave me a simple yet profound response: "Sometimes we are so busy talking *about* Jesus Christ that we forget to talk *with* him."

That sound you hear? That's the sound of my heart skipping a beat while the nail is hit firmly on the head. You see, I'm ashamed to admit it, but this priest was exactly right. All too often, I skip my morning prayer in order to head straight to the blog, check that day's articles, and inadvertently begin my workday. "Work is my prayer today, God," I justify to myself. "These posts will lead folks closer to you. We can't be late with the editorial schedule. I'll pray later." And later becomes tomorrow, or on Sunday morning, or "If I ever find a spare moment to breathe, Lord."

My days are best when my yes to the things I believe to the core of my being is more than a whispered, memorized offering on the way down to the coffee pot. As I have aged, fruitful morning prayer sets a rhythm for my days that has become increasingly important for my spiritual health. With little ones this was a challenge, but somehow I made it a priority most days. Now, as an empty nester, so frequently on the road, morning prayer is a way to ground myself, to remain connected to the timeless seasons of the divine, to feel at home spiritually wherever it is that I wake up.

As a part of my morning ritual, I include a few traditions. My best days begin with Lauds from the Liturgy of the Hours, the daily gospel reading from Mass, readings on the life of a saint or holy man or woman, and a remembrance of the intentions on my prayer list. I hold close to my heart my guys, Greg, Eric, and Adam—begging God to protect them and to help them to find his perfect joy in their days. My list always includes my and Greg's parents, our extended families, and the various prayer intentions of friends and readers from around the country who have requested support in times of illness, struggle, or strife.

Sometimes the weight of those intentions is a burden. I have been moved to tears on more than one occasion when I ponder so many people with such great needs. They write me daily, sharing their illnesses, the deaths of their loved ones, their unemployment or marital woes, and their faith crises. In those moments, I find peace in giving it all to God—the only one who hears and knows each and every pain, every tear. "Take the burdens, Lord," I beg. "Take the hurt, the loss, the fear, the anxiety. Replace them with your light, your joy, your love."

The aspect of my prayer life that perhaps needs the most emphasis mirrors part of my everyday communication style that also needs the most improvement: my ability to sit quietly and to listen. I'm pretty effective at delivering my side of a prayer conversation, but what I desire more fully in radically believing is a heart that is open to hearing his voice, his will, his desires most perfectly. A generous believer—just as a generous friend must do—needs to focus more on the art of hearing than on the delivery of a monologue.

My heart yearns for the stillness and grace to simply sit in silence, to quiet the noise in my brain, and to clear the space for God to enter the depths of my soul.

Jesus, I trust in you.
I believe. Help me in my disbelief.
I am yours.

Why Evangelize?

Have you ever sat after dinner in a beautiful restaurant and finished a fine meal with good friends? The waitress brings your dessert, a chocolate concoction too big for any one person, with multiple spoons. You take the first bite and the taste explodes in your mouth while your friends sit politely in their disciplined restraint. "Try this," you coax them. "It's absolutely perfect." Your friends, the kind who run marathons and strictly watch their diets, politely decline. "You *have* to try it," you needle them. "You've never tasted anything like this!" You don't give up until they finally reach for one of the extra spoons and dip in for the tiniest sliver of the confection. Before long, everyone at the table has a spoon and is gleefully agreeing that their life would not have been the same had they not joined you in eating the chocolate volcano. Your joy in sharing something you have a passion for is complete.

If we can share our passion for a slab of cake with this much conviction, why is it often so excruciatingly difficult to share our beliefs? Is a relationship with the One who formed us not the most amazing gift our generous hearts could ever give? And why is it even harder to do this with our family and best friends? Indeed, in my own life, I have found that it is easier to stand and give a testimonial in front of a room of a thousand strangers than it is to talk about faith topics with some of my closest relatives around the dinner table.

If my beliefs define me, if my yes is at the heart of my being, why do I hold back in sharing it with those I love most? Lately I have been praying to strengthen my ability to share my faith more perfectly by witnessing with my actions and with a joy of spirit. I want my loved ones to look at my life and to desire the secret ingredient that fuels me. I don't say this out of vanity, because in so many ways, I am flawed. But when folks ask me, "How do you do it all?" I'd like to respond with utter conviction that it's my belief in God that strengthens me for the challenges I face each day.

The third chapter of First Peter gives biblical words to this sensation I carry in my heart. We are called to "always be ready" to give a reason for the hope we feel but to do this with gentleness and respect. In the same way that I wouldn't take that chocolate lava cake and cram it down my friends' throats, I must be tender and deliberate in sharing my beliefs with others. But I need to avoid letting my caution become my excuse.

Saint Francis is credited with having said, "Preach the Gospel at all times and, when necessary, use words." This has become my favorite pep talk for the New Evangelization. This simple sentiment is profoundly perfect for teaching us how to more generously share the grace of our beliefs with everyone we meet. As we endeavor to live more perfectly as people of generous spirit, the virtue and grace of saying yes to belief needs to be at the heart of our every prayer, deed, and act of service.

To Ponder

1. What experience in your life has signaled a yes to knowing and accepting God's love for you?

2. If faith is "the realization of what is hoped for," what does true faith look like in your life? For what have you most deeply hoped, and how has God provided?

3. What logical and emotional constraints keep you from fully trusting God?

4. How is your belief in God witnessed in word and deed?

5. Who are the people in your life that draw you more fully into a yes relationship with God and his bountiful love?

6. What aspects of your faith life need to be renewed with greater vigor?

7. How is your life a living testament to the truths you believe?

Let us pray.

Heavenly Father, source and summit of all good,
I want to believe in you with all my heart,
to know and love you fully to the depths of my soul.
So often, I fall short. I doubt, I compromise,
I profess with words but my actions belie.

Be at my side and in my heart today
as I journey toward you.
May my yes to your love be unwavering,
undaunted by life's daily busyness and strife.

May my zeal for you spread to all I meet,
that they, too, may fully know the depths
of your endless grace.

May I sense intimately your perfect peace in my heart
today and always, praising you as a believer
with a life that aims to echo the bounty of your gifts.
Amen.

2. The Grace *of* Generativity

Greg is a detail-oriented neat freak, and I'm a busy slob. He is the definition of proactive planning, while I am a born procrastinator. And while I wear my heart on my sleeve, his emotional life is deeply interior and far more private. Yet, somehow, on most things, we meet happily in the middle with a constant recommitment to our life-long partnership. There is no human relationship in my life that means more to me than my marriage. Every day, in every way, I endeavor to give myself fully to what we are and have together.

Loving Greg is a daily decision, a yes that has been—and continues to be—the most blessed choice of my life. Ours was a love affair that sprouted at a tender age and has happily blossomed over more than half a lifetime—nearly thirty years spent in one another's arms. When I hear the words "unconditional love," I immediately see Greg, who has loved me through early years when we were discovering one another inside and out and into middle age when we can now complete each other's thoughts in unspoken communications that convey the enormity of our connection.

Learning to give myself generously in love is a skill that is as old as it is new. The joy and the challenge of journeying with a partner for life is found in the unending twists and turns that constitute the voyage. At times, we're partners on a tandem bicycle, pedaling in unison. Of course at other times, the two of us squish into a dinghy and row against one another, going nowhere but in circles. If you're married, you understand this.

Our daily yeses have passed by in a blur of being poor newlyweds, uncertain parents, and now new empty nesters. We've been through financial ups and downs, stressful career turns, and teenage drivers. And somehow, the tests that have presented themselves along our path draw me ever closer to Greg. At the center of our incredible bond is a loving God who has consecrated us fully to one another and who continues to cement our love through happiness and strife.

For me the most daunting challenge in our marriage has been the discrepancy in how we each express our faith. A cradle Catholic who never questioned God or his centrality within my Church, I met and married a nominally-raised Protestant not truly committed to any faith tradition. But I'm almost wise enough now to recognize that because we love our God differently—and, perhaps more importantly, that we express that love differently—doesn't mean that one of us was or is right and the other wrong. We are different that's all.

Perhaps you find yourself similarly challenged when it comes to fully giving yourself in love. You may shelter a small portion of your heart (or a big one), shielding yourself from true intimacy because of crevices in your relationship that divide rather than unify you. As I did with the different faith expressions in my marriage, you may fear that it is safer to accept the status quo and leave emotions unshared rather than rock an otherwise stable vessel. If you find yourself nodding as you read this, I encourage you to take a step forward in confidence and more generously give of yourself in this relationship. When we withhold our true feelings out of fear, we place constraints upon God's capacity for incredible mercy and compassion. We block the healing that he wants to bring us. We nurse our own wounds without inviting the divine physician to assist in the treatment.

Once Greg and I were able to venture beyond what I considered a "don't ask, don't tell" pact in our marriage, I began to trust in the belief that God desired deeper unity—true communion—for the two of us. I place the blame squarely on me and my own doubts for not fully giving myself to our union for many years. As I have witnessed Greg's strong, quiet spiritual life blossom over the years, I have loved him in a way I never imagined possible.

Most Sunday mornings we sit separately at church, since Greg is now involved in our music ministry. In that space of a moment when I watch from afar as Greg goes forward to receive Communion, I'm reminded of the words Saint Monica spoke to her son Augustine at the time of his conversion: "Son, nothing in this world now affords me delight. I do not know what there is now for me to do or why I am still here, all my hopes in this world being now fulfilled." My desire for the salvation of my soul mate is as great as my own hope in Jesus Christ.

Bending So We Don't Break

My parents have long had a wonderful saying: "Never leave one good party in search of another." Of course, the adage applied to real parties. My mom and dad were notorious for being the last to leave any social gathering. They were the first on the dance floor and the last to wave goodbye, usually after having stayed around to help clean up.

But I learned early on that their wisdom also applied to most of the important things in life: education, career, and especially marriage. When I need an example of a strong marriage, I simply look to my own parents, who have been going strong for fifty years and counting. I won't say that they never fought, but I will say that they were partners through and through. At the core of their relationship is a mutual covenant to help one another get to heaven and to experience heaven on earth within our family.

From them, I have learned what marriage is and is not.

- My marriage is not a team of two individuals but rather a melding of two hearts making mutual sacrifices toward common goals.

- My marriage is not the total giving up of myself and who I am but rather the lifelong journey toward a better version of the partner I desire to be.

- My marriage is training myself to stop thinking in terms of "I" and "me" and to consider at every turn "us" and "we."

- My marriage doesn't mean that I have to spend every waking moment with Greg, but it should lead toward a constantly greater sense of desiring his company—physically and emotionally.

- My marriage isn't always easy or pretty or perfect, but striving to be the best wife I can possibly be should always be at the top of my priorities. She is the person God desires me to be, making the most of the gifts and talents he has created within me. When I give my very best to Greg and he gives his best to me, we are closest to living out the perfection of the walk with Christ to which Baptism calls us.

Marriage has taught me the art of compromise—movement toward agreement in disputes by moving toward mutual concessions. Author Phyllis McGinley once wrote, "Compromise, if not the spice of life, is its solidity. It is what makes nations great and marriages happy."

My marital yes has been a gradual learning of what it means to consider life through a prism shared with another individual with his own set of needs, desires, and priorities. In order to reach compromise, I find myself constantly working to better my communication skills and to avoid the assumption that my husband is a mind reader. How can Greg reach a shared goal with me if he has no idea what my desires or needs are? But far too often, in my selfish way, I have chosen not to verbalize and instead to penalize, holding it over my partner's head when things don't go my way.

In my marriage, "Never leave one good party in search of another" shines the light not only on our fidelity but also on the joy that I desire to build with Greg at the heart of our marriage. Sticking with one another through ramen-noodle poverty days, crazed parenting of toddlers and teens, and the current turning toward our middle-aged and senior years hasn't always been pretty or fun. We have made our fair share of bad judgments along the way. But I will honestly proclaim that at the end of the day and the end of my life, I want to be found in the company of my very best friend, my husband, my party-partner for life.

Yes to Our Family

Despite being raised in a big family, I did not come to motherhood with a yearning or a great desire for our firstborn, Eric. In a way, I am ashamed to admit that when I took the home-pregnancy test one Friday evening in 1991, I cried when I saw the results. How horrible, right?!

Greg and I had been married for approximately five years when we decided that the timing was right to begin sharing our lives with children. And while we came to this readiness after conversation and prayer, I was surrounded at that time by friends who were struggling with infertility. I somehow thought that even though we were "ready," it would take me a few years to conceive and I would have some time to cultivate the maternal instincts I knew I was sorely lacking at that age.

I look back now and shudder at the woman I was then, so wrapped up in my career and my personal goals that I couldn't conceive of sharing my time with children. How shortsighted, how selfish, and how wrong I was to think that in opening our hearts, lives, and home to a baby, I would be giving up the things that I thought most mattered to me. Blessedly, Greg was just the companion I needed to enter this phase of life that scared the pants off of me. My uncertainty was matched by his confidence and surety. He was ready to be a father.

Our little Eric came during Greg's third year of residency. I planned to deliver our child and to return to work—to a career I deeply valued. But all that changed when I began looking for child-care arrangements. Greg and I realized that something would have to give. Both of our schedules and commitments had us working so many hours, often including irregular schedules and weekends. My "retiring" to care full time for Eric was initially a compromise, and I was not the mom who spent hours creating the perfect layette or was a natural at breastfeeding. But somehow our Eric survived my insufficiencies, and he thrived.

When I look back at our "babymoon" period, I know that even with the dirty diapers and the sleepless nights, I was falling in love with a side of my husband that I had never seen before. With Eric, and again with little Adam, Greg developed at once a tenderness and a leadership for our band that made me feel both loved and utterly cared for. At every point in the raising of our little clan, I have considered our partnership strengthened and renewed by his utter devotion to our family.

As much as I grew to love being a mom, the temporary walk away from a career that had truly come to define me left me struggling to discover who I was other than Greg's wife and Eric and Adam's mom. I love and readily embrace both of those titles, yet there is a fine line we traverse when we endeavor to give the very best of ourselves to our loved ones without losing ourselves in the process.

How easy it was to congratulate myself for an A on one child's spelling test and to deride myself for another young boy's name on the chalkboard because he was in trouble. How strong the compulsion to recite my own now-cobwebbed résumé when standing next to my husband with his colleagues at a party or social event. How shortsighted of me not to realize that my yes to being a wife and mother was truly a commitment to the things that mattered the very most in my life, despite what others thought. How blind I was, thinking that I needed to glamorize or exaggerate the way I spent my days.

It's easy to look back now and try to rewrite some of the chapters of our family history to fit the picture-perfect version of myself that I wish our boys would remember. I'd like them to forget my impatience, my nagging, and my selfishness, replacing those faults with chocolate-chip-cookie-scented snapshots of a well-appointed home decorated with the arts and crafts we'd created together at the kitchen table. But that's not how it was.

In retrospect, I see that our loving path to parenthood was uniquely our own, based on our family's individual circumstances and our personal charisms. The years with our sons at home passed by in a blur of sports teams and homework assignments, first dates and college applications. I wish I could have slowed them down, done some things less selfishly, and taken more time to simply sit and snuggle with my babies or take long walks with my teens. But I wouldn't change the unit we have become. We are awesome and our mutual yes is to family and faith, first and foremost. With our boys now independent young men and perched on futures of their own, I continue to see the evolution of our particular flavor of parental love.

Moments of letting go are often as heart-wrenchingly challenging as our babies' first bad falls or their first broken hearts. Most of us moms and dads can recall a time when we knew every hair on our children's heads, the way a curl of their lips meant an ensuing burst of emotions, or just what spot to tickle to melt them into a bundle of giggles. Now my sons are both geographically distant and emotionally their own men. Today, my yes as a mom means avoiding the urge to cyber-stalk, to make their decisions for them, or to wish them back into the nest. These struggles of parenthood call me to say yes to the grace of love and generativity.

Now more than ever, I identify with Mother Mary, whose yes to love meant not only giving birth to God's son but also giving him over to a destiny that meant so very much grief and pain. As parents, we desire more than anything to shield our beloved children from any harm or hurt. But overprotecting them keeps them from coming to the fullness of life that God created for them. Our generous giving means pulling back, submitting to God's plan, and always maintaining a steady stream of loving prayer and a home where we welcome them back with open arms on their terms, not our own.

Selfless Love

Ask me whom I love and I will begin a long list that begins with Greg, Eric, Adam, my immediate family and Greg's, and extends to seemingly countless friends for whom I have a profound love. The Greek word *agape*, used in the New Testament to describe the kind of love to which Jesus calls his disciples, can be defined as "the selfless love one person has for another without sexual implications, especially love that is spiritual in nature."

Agape is a love that is more concerned with giving than taking, with caring for rather than being cared about. This mutual selflessness and generosity is at the core of any good marriage. And it is the ingredient that bonds us to any number of other friends in our lives.

Living out a truly selfless love means considering in our relationships how we give the best of ourselves to serving those around us. Pause an instant to formulate a list of three people—not family—whom you truly love. Ask yourself why. Why do you love these people? Be honest.

Perhaps your list looks a bit like mine:

- Martha, a trusted spiritual mentor. Her faith and her generosity are boundless.

- Mara, a true companion. I can share any problem with her and she will listen without judgment.

- Sarah, who challenges me and gives me hope. Her gifts complement mine, and we make a terrific team.

Upon prayerful consideration of my list of beloved friends, it's clear to me that my initial reaction as to why I love Martha, Mara, and Sarah has far too much to do with what I gain from these relationships. Rather than seeing these friendships as love for beautiful souls—each created, albeit unique in their own fashions, by God in his image—my first impulse is to identify how our friendship benefits me. Perhaps this is a common flaw in the way we as a society think about love. If you're of a certain age, you'll remember a famous movie scene in which Tom Cruise's character Jerry Maguire ended a protracted speech to his beloved with the now-famous words, "You complete me." How very often in my life have I surrounded myself with friends who "complete" the parts of myself I see as shortcomings. Instead of standing in awe of the friends I named above for the simple fact that they are of God, his beautiful creations and an image of his divine love, I err by reflecting on our relationships as though through a mirror, aimed squarely at my own ego.

Ask yourself what you give selflessly to the three people you have listed. If this part of the exercise is a challenge to us, then we have some work to do to get to the true yes of selfless love. The gospels are full of teachings on the nature of love. Some of these provide us with clarity about how to give of ourselves. One of the most poignant directives comes to us through Jesus' teaching to his disciples at the Last Supper. He exhorts his closest friends: "I give you a new commandment: Love one another. As I have loved you, so you also should love one another. This is how all will know that you are my disciples, if you have love for one another" (Jn 13:34–35). This oft-quoted advice is sandwiched between two scriptural signs of how profoundly a love relationship can be broken—the betrayal of Christ by Judas and the prediction of Peter's denial.

Like Judas and Peter, we can at times flip from blissful love for our friends to selfish protection of our own interests. Agape, selfless at its core, is turned on end by our "what's in it for me" attitude. Throughout John's first epistle, we encounter reminders that true agape is mutually beneficial:

> Whoever loves his brother remains in the light, and there is nothing in him to cause a fall. (1 Jn 2:10)

> We know that we have passed from death to life because we love our brothers. Whoever does not love remains in death. (1 Jn 3:14)

> Beloved, let us love one another, because love is of God; everyone who loves is begotten by God and knows God. Whoever is without love does not know God, for God is love. (1 Jn 4:7–8)

> If anyone says, "I love God," but hates his brother, he is a liar; for whoever does not love

> a brother whom he has seen cannot love God
> whom he has not seen. (1 Jn 4:20)

Beyond pretty words, John's teachings on love come from a heart that knew and lived agape. John was called the "beloved disciple," and among the disciples, it was he alone who stood with Mary at the foot of Christ's cross, watching his beloved friend and teacher be put to death. It was John who took Mary into his home and cared for her. It was John who raced when he heard of the Resurrection to meet his risen Lord and he who gave the rest of his days to share the Good News—a living testament to his love for Jesus.

If in our own lives we lack the love of someone like John—a friend who would give his or her all to stand by our side in our moments of crisis—we may be tempted to throw up our hands and confess that such love is impossible. But rather than giving up, I challenge each of us, myself first and foremost, to become bearers of the selfless love we so desire.

Think again about your list of three trusted friends, as I recall mine. Do we hold ourselves accountable to the "beloved disciple" standard of love? Ask yourself:

- Am I a constant emotional companion to my friend, or am I simply present when it is convenient?

- Do I stand with my loved one in moments of greatest need?

- Does my heart leap at the sight of my loved one in recognition of God's presence?

If our honest responses have us reeling, let's make today the day we begin to actively employ a fully generous attitude in our relationships. Let's reclaim the moniker *friend* from a simple action on a social network and turn it into a decision, a declaration, a sacred mission.

If the Apostle John is too distant a role model for you, it may be helpful to dwell for a few moments on modern-day portraits of selfless love in our day.

- Thomas and Natalie had only been married a few short months when he sustained a severe, life-threatening injury. His new bride became a life partner in ways the two could never have anticipated. Their loving support of one another through a time of intense trial has been a witness to friends literally around the globe who have prayed with them during Thomas's recovery. Far from victims, they are masters of the true meaning of unconditional love.

- Lisa and Tim have opened their hearts and homes to foster children, battling to provide these young ones with a sense of security and peace amid challenging life circumstances. Their desire to become a "forever family" for a child in need shines a light on what it truly means to parent.

- Blessed Mother Teresa of Calcutta, although no longer with us, continues to leave the world a legacy of love. For her, who said, "Spread love everywhere you go. Let no one ever come to you without leaving happier," loving the most vulnerable in society was a tangible way of better loving God.

When we look at the world around us with yes-to-love eyes, it is easier to see everyday sightings of agape at work. If the scars of cynicism have begun to crust our hearts, we must challenge ourselves to not only look for portraits of selfless love each day but also indeed to paint our own.

Claiming Generativity

As I settle into my fifties, *generativity* is a concept that seems to be increasingly on my mind. Perhaps, this is a middle-aged fruit of a lifetime devoted to getting better at loving others. According to *Merriam-Webster*, the word means "a concern for people besides self and family that usually develops during middle age; *especially*: a need to nurture and guide younger people and contribute to the next generation. . . ."

Pope Francis recently shared about an act of generativity when he responded with a phone call to a young man who had sent him a letter: "I realized that he was a young man who is growing, that he saw in me a father, and that the letter tells something of his life to that father. The father cannot say, 'I do not care.' This type of fruitfulness is so good for me."

In the 1950s, psychoanalyst Erik Erikson coined the term *generativity* and defined it as "the concern in establishing and guiding the next generation." He explored generativity versus stagnation as the seventh phase in his theory of psychosocial development. Coming in adulthood and marked by the basic virtue of caring, Erikson believed that functioning adults in the middle phases of life look to create a lasting legacy by creating

or nurturing things or people that would outlast themselves. As such, he saw parenthood as one means of
being generative, as opposed to stagnating.

At this time in my life, when I begin to feel the
tug of generativity pulling at most of my significant
life decisions, I find that it is precisely the seeds of love
that cause me to be most motivated in legacy leaving.
The love I feel for my sons prompts me to nurture their
happy, healthy, and holy transition to adulthood. I am
less concerned with how much money they will earn
and more concerned with the joy they will feel as they
impact the world around them.

The love I feel for colleagues prompts me to continually look for ways to build up and nurture their professional and spiritual growth. This sort of generativity
is most present for me in the interactions I have with
our writers at CatholicMom.com. As I pen this book,
our ranks of contributing bloggers—all volunteers who
share their gifts freely and with great dedication—number more than one hundred fifty. For our writers, I desire
that they have the opportunity to shine. The best parts of
my workdays are the moments I spend mentoring and
encouraging young writers who are in the early phases
of discovering their voices in written word.

The love I feel for my friends in the community
where I live prompts me to be a better friend, a more
responsible neighbor, and a stronger supporter of initiatives that make the place in which I live a more cohesive
and enlivening environment.

Generativity mandates that we set aside selfish
interests in our love relationships. It means considering more often what we can give rather than what we

will gain. At its most genuine, generativity plants a pay-it-forward seed that, when nurtured, takes on a life so much greater than the one we will live in our days on earth. But to be that fruitful, sincere generativity must be unconcerned with how what we leave behind will cause others to remember us. Instead, lasting generativity takes self-interest out of the equation.

The fact that I've arrived at this understanding of and desire for generativity so late in my life is one of my regrets. For so many years, my concept of love dwelt too greatly on self-satisfaction. And even now I have too many days when "What's in it for me?" is my mantra.

On days when we get this right, love means passionate, profound, secure attachment that is at its very core life-affirming, life-giving, and generative. It is this goal that will drive our giving generously of ourselves in all the relationships that sustain us in this life.

To Ponder

1. What early life events shaped your concept of what a generous love relationship looks like?

2. How do your spiritual leanings shape the way you love?

3. What are some ways in which you "bend" in love relationships?

4. Who in your experience are examples of selfless love that you might emulate?

5. What role does generativity play in the way you love those closest to you?

Let us pray.

Lord, lover of us all,
you are present in every moment of every day.
Your love gave, sacrificed, taught, and ultimately saved.
I yearn to love in a way that seeks foremost to give,
less often to take.
Help me to follow your example, Lord,
to give of myself completely and without an agenda,
to affirm, build up, console,
and understand my loved ones,
to be wholly present to their needs,
and to be always appreciative of and authentically open to
their gifts.
May the love I shower on those around me be life-giving,
warmed by sincere affection and joy.
Amen.

3. The Grace *of* Creativity

Not long ago as I worked with a small faith-sharing group of young moms, one of them asked what I had studied in college and how it had led me to where I am today in my work. We all laughed when I told them that my undergraduate major at Notre Dame was French. While it may seem as though I was simply a party girl shopping for a husband, I was in fact following sound advice my dad had given me: "Study what you love."

My undergraduate studies built on my passion for communication and travel and led me to a graduate degree in human-resource development. A vibrant career in health-care recruiting and training followed. However, my very first post-college job was far from glamorous. I was a file clerk in a personnel office working for $5.10 an hour. Nearly broke, newly married with a medical-student spouse to feed—and proud bearer of that awesome French degree—I took the first job I could land. I remember the party Greg and I threw the day I got my first raise and my salary was increased to $5.35 an hour. That was big money in our little one-bedroom apartment on the bad side of the Nashville tracks in 1986.

Young and inexperienced as I was, I had been taught and happily followed my parents' advice to give my best to whatever I was doing. They were convinced that studying what you loved would result in good grades and high academic achievement, which would eventually result in a solid, satisfying career. Within a short time of taking that first real job, I was promoted from the files to recruiting and then ultimately to managing the office that held the files and the recruiters. Along the way, I took advantage of my employer's offer to pay for half of my graduate-school education. The day Greg graduated from medical school, I happily earned my master's degree in human-resource development, having studied part time in a weekend executive program while I worked full time. Interestingly, the communication skills I honed with my French degree combined with the presentation and writing skills I acquired in graduate school formed a solid base for exactly the work I find myself doing now in my second career.

At the time, I didn't recognize the giving of myself that was involved in all those long hours of work topped with tests and papers. I was simply pursuing a passion for work I loved. I won't say that I was extraordinarily motivated by filing for eight hours a day, but I kept my eyes on the prize, worked diligently, and saw the connection that an advanced degree could have in achieving the career goals I held. That degree led the way to a wonderful corporate position when we moved to California as Greg entered his residency program in emergency medicine. With both of our careers in full bloom, the extra hours we worked didn't feel like drudgery. We were both doing what we loved.

There were definitely days when I felt tired, overworked, and undervalued. That happens even in the best of jobs. But I could visualize the trajectory of my work and could see the path I wanted to travel to the destination I desired. I had big plans, but they largely revolved around selfish interests: rank, salary, and reputation.

Along Came Eric

We hadn't arranged for childcare before Eric's birth, and after he came along it was immediately clear to me that given our work circumstances, we weren't a good prospect to be a dual-career family. Greg wasn't going to quit his residency program, so mine was the job we gave up, and I became a stay-at-home mother, begrudgingly. I remember vividly the day I was supposed to have returned to work. That early January morning found me not back at my desk but with our little one in tow at my first meeting with a moms group at the local YWCA. When I was invited to introduce myself to the group, I got only one or two words into "I'm Lisa and . . ." before I burst into tears.

Who was I, anyway? In the past, I would have said, "I'm the area recruitment manager. I earned my master's at Vanderbilt and manage twelve employees at a tertiary care hospital . . ." But now all I could muster was, "I'm Eric's mom."

It took me a long time to embrace the fact that giving myself generously to the vocation of being wife and mother was certainly the most important career decision I would ever make. If we measure our work by my favorite definition—an activity involving mental or physical effort done in order to achieve a purpose or result—I could toil a lifetime and never find a finer way to say yes to God's plan for my life.

An amazing by-product of the decision that began as a temporary compromise is that being Eric and Adam's mom and Greg's wife led me to a second professional career I could honestly never have imagined. As I told the moms at that recent fellowship gathering, had I set out in my younger years to accomplish even a part of what I've been blessed to do in the past decade, it might never have happened. I credit God's grace and the ingenuity of his imagination for leading me to the place I now find myself in life. I can look back now at the baby steps that led to the professional work in which I am now immersed, and I can see forks in the path, places where a yes led in one direction and away from another at exactly the right moment. I give the glory to God for opening doors, pointing the way, and over and over again graciously accepting my yes.

Giving Oneself Over to the Work

The smartest thing work-wise that I do every day is to include among my morning prayers a plea to accurately hear and respond to God's agenda for my work. Most days, when I'm already working on my mental to-do list before my feet hit the floor, those prayers honestly include a chiding of God for not having ordained a more worthy captain of the little ship I'm steering with my work. But then I offer him my private consent to his plans—not Lisa's—for what will become of my day. And especially on the days when frustration, obstacles, exhaustion, or confusion plague me, I pray overtime to be obedient to that yes.

At times I am like a petulant two-year-old, throwing a fit in the middle of the room. "Seriously, God!" I rail. "Why can't I just give up and have a regular life?" And then I laugh at myself and at the concept that *anyone's* life or work is ever that simple.

And that's where the grace of giving myself generously to my work enters in. The grace of that particular "Yes, Lord" means being someone who:

- **prays always for God's will to be done in and through her.** Regardless of our life's work, we all have divine purpose. But ascertaining and accepting God's purpose for our work means seeking his will above our own.

- **is grateful for every opportunity,** even (or perhaps especially) the hidden ones that run counter to our plans. A spirit of gratitude translates obstacles into second chances or a way to see new and unique visions of our work.

- **asks for help and graciously accepts it.** This is a challenge to those of us who like self-sufficiency. It's perhaps more of a challenge when we have help foisted upon us without asking for it. Next time you're tempted to decline an offer of help, pause, recognize the lifeline God is throwing you, then shut up and take it. You'll be amazed by what happens.

- **pays attention to minute details.** Paying attention to all components of a work project, but perhaps most importantly the foundational details, indicates a precision and a pride in one's product that gives respect and diligence to the task at hand.

- **sees success as a gift and grasps for it.** Being successful is not a sin. Being vain is. With an attitude that places a premium upon cultivating a generous spirit, success sets you up to offer even more moments of graceful giving to the people with whom you work.

- **leaves a legacy that doesn't self-aggrandize.** Rarely is a work success an individual accomplishment. Our work bears the most fruit when it is generative (Remember that word?) and when it builds upon itself for the good of the team, the organization, society, and our world.

Peeling It to Perfection

One of my greatest desires for my work is that it be of God and pleasing to God. This means endeavoring to give my best to the task at hand, even when I find it boring or displeasing. While I'm far from perfect, living generously in this realm of my life means striving for the very best and learning from the inevitable ways in which I fall short of that standard.

This is an attitude that my parents passed along to me, and one I hope Greg and I have conveyed to our sons. When I was a teen, one of our family's favorite movies was the classic *Chariots of Fire*. There are a few lines in the film that have long stuck with me. They pertain perfectly to the grace of this unique giving of ourselves and our gifts to the work we do. Rev. James Liddell, the father of the main character, Olympic runner Eric Liddell, says to his son:

> You can praise God by peeling a spud if
> you peel it to perfection. Don't compromise.
> Compromise is a language of the devil. Run
> in God's name and let the world stand back
> and in wonder.

How beautiful is his reminder that all work has an inherent dignity! It is crucial for us as people of faith to realize that for us to do justice to our vocations—regardless of the nature of our work—we must "peel to perfection." Shortly after this moment of fatherly encouragement, the movie portrays Eric Liddell, post-race, standing in a thunderstorm and passionately preaching the Word of God. With a perfect Scottish brogue and charm, he delivers this testimonial:

> You came to see a race today. To see someone
> win. It happened to be me. But I want you to

do more than just watch a race. I want you
to take part in it. I want to compare faith to
running in a race. It's hard. It requires concentration of will, energy of soul. . . .

Everyone runs in her own way, or his own
way. And where does the power come from,
to see the race to its end? From within. Jesus
said, "Behold, the Kingdom of God is within
you. If with all your hearts, you truly seek me,
you shall ever surely find me." If you commit
yourself to the love of Christ, then that is how
you run a straight race.

Liddell, who went on to live a missionary life after
his successful athletic career, is a "yes mentor" whom
I ponder frequently. In using his gifts as an athlete, he
never lost sight of his Christian values, even refusing to
race in the Olympics on the Sabbath when it conflicted
with the practice of his faith. He was able to tap into the
same inner strength that can fuel the rest of us when we
strive to give our very best to the task at hand. It's that
light of Christ within each of us that helps us to run our
straight race, to peel our spud to perfection, and as such
to glorify the God who created us just as we are.

When Work Doesn't Come

Some of you will read this and think me bold for sharing my privileged occupation and my satisfaction with
my work. You may be struggling with the same stress
a good friend of mine experienced recently when she
went through a period of extended unemployment. This
friend is a top-notch professional who—through no fault

of her own—suddenly found herself out of work for well over a year. Hers was a perfect résumé. There was no good reason for her situation other than too few jobs in her chosen field.

I've never personally been in that situation, and I can only begin to imagine just how painful the cross must be to bear. I imagine that the temptation to succumb to despair must be huge. To offer a bit of support for those readers who deal with this burden, I turned to trusted friends who have recently experienced the challenge of unemployment or underemployment. Their advice was consistent in a way that comes from a "been there, done that" perspective.

Among their suggestions were practical hints, including volunteering in your selected field, which may lead to employment; retraining in a new and more in-demand career; and taking a less-attractive job while you continue your long-term search. Many friends underscored the need to humbly ask friends, family, and previous colleagues for assistance in the search. They suggested overcoming false pride that might stand in the way of accepting or even asking for help meeting basic needs and scrupulously controlling what you spend. Networking, especially in today's competitive job market, seemed to be essential. Advance preparation, consistent attention to even the smallest details of the search, and involvement in one's community were also recurrent themes.

Even more inspirational was the attitudinal advice offered by friends who have had to hit the pavement and fill out far too many employment applications. For them, an active prayer life and intercessory prayer

partners were lifelines. They advocated for both per-
sistence (without being obnoxious) and maintaining
a positive attitude, even when the situation seemed to
merit negativity. Most of the individuals who responded
to my inquiry urged flexibility and openness to new or
previously considered career paths. The call for a long-
term, big-picture view and an optimistic attitude was
nearly universal.

From two of the friends I queried on this topic, I
received terrific insights that seem very yes-oriented.
Don shared:

> What you do to earn a living is different from
> who you are. Everyone needs to sell some-
> thing in order to earn a living. For employees,
> that means selling what you do during your
> time at work. What you sell is not who you
> are. If you're unemployed, it may just be that
> no one at the moment wants to buy what you
> are selling. That could mean that you need
> to change what it is you sell because no one
> needs that anymore. Or it could mean that
> there just isn't enough demand for it for the
> time being. Either way, it is not a rejection of
> who you are, as much as it might feel that
> way. You are a child of God, deserving of
> human dignity, regardless of whether or not
> someone wants to buy what you do.

And from Alexis, the friend mentioned above, the one
who eventually landed the perfect job, in the perfect
place, on God's time schedule, one last tip:

Don't let others tell you who you are. Trust that the Holy Spirit, living within you, is who created you. Know where you belong and what you were created for. Wait for the right position to resonate with what gifts and talents you have. Offer yourself daily to the Creator of the universe and ask him to make up what is missing and create and re-create you if needed. When the world speaks of reinventing yourself, know that you are not of this world, and you must let the one who invented you do a new great thing in you for the very place where you will bring glory to his name. He's your first boss, your headhunter, waymaker, negotiator, and mediator. He is the builder, and unless the Lord builds the house, he who labors, labors in vain.

Creativity—Channeling God's Imagination

Creativity has never been one of my strong suits. I so greatly admire friends and colleagues who have the ingenuity to dream big and as such to not place limits around God's capacity to amaze. I'm better at taking a dream someone else has created and making pieces of it happen, and I'm more at ease coloring within the lines someone else has drawn.

Lately, I've realized that by assuming I lack creativity, I am not giving a full yes in my work. When my big-idea moments are followed by sixteen "buts," I stymie the Creator of all. I place limits on the boundless potential God has planted within me.

I have a friend who is the polar opposite of me in this way. He is an absolute idea person. He has so many ideas that he often leaves his fellow team members wondering about his capacity to actually follow through on even half of what he dreams up. At times, I've looked at this person and thought he should get a better handle on his creative juices. But more recently, I've been in absolute wonder at his incredible generosity of spirit in fully giving himself to the dreams that God surely has for him.

A dictionary.com definition of the word *creativity* describes perfectly this friend's capacity to brainstorm: "The ability to transcend traditional ideas, rules, patterns, relationships, or the like, and to create meaningful new ideas, forms, methods, etc.; originality, progressiveness, or imagination."

When we open ourselves to the potential of the creative forces within us, we unleash our power to be more meaningful in our work, to leave an enhanced legacy, and to make our world a better place. With new ideas, we can often reach more people and help them to grow closer to being the persons God intends them to be.

One of my weekly jobs is to serve as a technology contributor for a radio station, which causes me to marvel at God's sense of humor, since I've learned most of what I know about tech from *For Dummies* books, by Googling, or at the University of YouTube. The radio host and I work together to identify a tech story that is in the news and to apply a faith-oriented spin to the topic. Having done this for a few years now, I find myself increasingly fascinated by the capacity humans have to create—to come up with ingenious new ways to do even the most mundane tasks. A recent example of bold creative thinking is Amazon's new Prime Air project. The project calls for unmanned drones called octocopters to be used for delivering small packages to users within a ten-mile area in fewer than thirty minutes—from keyboard to your front door in less than the time it probably takes to have a pizza delivered.

When we examine this idea, it's easy to begin picking it apart and naming all the reasons it will never get off the ground. But let's ponder for a moment the genius of looking at an everyday task from a creative perspective. Examining the octocopter reminds us to look at the way in which we perform our daily tasks and to dream, to ponder, to create. Our yes to new ways of doing our work is more complete when we allot a portion of our time, energy, and daily prayer to visioning the future with fresh, open eyes.

If this comes as a challenge for you, as it does for me, please join me outside my comfort zone. When you plan your workweek, schedule in a period of time to create and to work through the implementation of your creations. Surround yourself with individuals who are open to and excel at letting their creative juices flow. Learn to immediately capture moments of ingenuity as they come to you. And pray for creativity—a fresh openness to God's ideas for your work.

Establishing a system for creativity may sound counterintuitive, but if we don't capture those inspired moments as they are given to us, we are more likely to lose them to the ether. I use an online system, accessible on all of my mobile tools as well as on the computer at my desk, to document and map out ideas and projects.

As silly as it may sound, I also keep a notebook next to my bed for those middle-of-the-night brainstorms that wake me from sleep. More than a few troublesome issues have been worked out in that notebook. Sometimes I have a hard time deciphering my scrawl the next morning, but I love to look back at those pages and see the birth of bright ideas that later came to fruition.

Creativity in our work is a generous gift of ourselves to work that opens our hearts and minds to the fullness of all God has dreamed for us. Opening the door to his will, even when it sounds far-fetched or outlandish, glorifies the ingenuity of the One whose potential knows no bounds.

Productivity Parables

If we're looking for role models to guide us in the generous giving of ourselves to our occupations, the Bible provides plenty of fodder for the argument that hard work should pave our path to heaven. Certainly, were she living in today's world, the woman of Proverbs 31, praised at the gates for the fruits of her labor, would be a coach for getting stuff done. Even as early as the first chapter of Genesis we find God setting man and woman in the Garden of Eden and calling them to care for and cultivate the world around them.

Solomon's song in Psalm 127 calls to heart God's place in our work:

> Unless the Lord build the house,
> they labor in vain who build.
> Unless the Lord guard the city,
> in vain does the guard keep watch.

> It is vain for you to rise early
> and put off your rest at night,
> To eat bread earned by hard toil—
> all this God gives to his beloved in sleep
> (Ps 127:1–2).

Our work is *of* God, *by* God, and undertaken *for* our God. Christ's parable of the talents in Matthew reminds us never to "bury" our gifts from God. And in the Second Letter to the Thessalonians, we read Paul's scolding of those who are too busy minding the business of others to do their own work. My favorite scriptural marching orders for giving ourselves generously to work that sings of God's endless bounty are found in Paul's Letter to the Colossians. Taped to the desk in my office is a small sticky note, coffee-stained and well-prayed over, reading: "And whatever you do, in word or in deed, do everything in the name of the Lord Jesus, giving thanks to God the Father through him" (3:17).

Yes happens best and most authentically in my work when I remember first and foremost why I do what I do and through whom I do it.

When It's Not Perfect

Will a yes to God's will for our work mean perfection? Not likely. I'm never perfect, and some days I let that be my excuse for withholding the best of myself from the God who's setting my agenda for life. In graduate school, a favorite professor of mine used to talk about "hound-winding" in our work. He described hound-winding as all of those machinations we go through when we're getting ready to take on a project or an initiative—like a dog circling her bed, tramping the sleep surface until it's just right.

As a writer, I hound-wind far too much, sometimes circling my work waiting for all the stars to align before I dive in. I tell myself that I must have the proper inspiration, the correct window of open time, an environment that is silent and conducive to concentration, and even my coffee heated to the perfect temperature.

Of course, since I typically live a chaotic life, those factors almost never present themselves all at once. Consequently, I use this as an excuse to procrastinate, and the more I procrastinate, the more my hound-winding keeps me from offering a fully productive giving of myself to my work. Knowing this tendency and trying to overcome it is a constant striving in me.

Striving for perfection in our work is a good thing. But when we do, we run the risks of comparing our work to the work of others and of measuring our accomplishments only by *what* we produce—the outcomes or end results. Perhaps what we are called to be perfect at is in *how* we go about our work. Maybe, as people of faith, we are to measure our accomplishments by the manner in which we work, nothing more. Are we doing our best today, with all we have at our disposal? Are we loving and just? Are we honest, fair, and honorable? In a most fundamental way, the work we do is to be done in such a way that others see at least a glimmer of God there. So if we mash potatoes or produce movies to earn money, we do so perfectly so long as God's goodness is made manifest in us. On any given day, you and I know whether or not the work we're doing is the very best we have to give and if we glorify God by the way in which we do it.

Life is really never perfect, is it? We all have to endure seasons in our work when we simply put our heads down, say a prayer, shut up, and get our jobs done. Perhaps it helps to realize that even those yes moments, when we feel work is drudgery, below us, or simply not a good fit for us, are precious in their own ways. Catholics reading this may recognize them as "offer it up" opportunities. "Offering it up" means making those less-than-perfect projects, assignments, duties, or jobs love offerings to God. In their own way, those "I'd rather not do this" tasks—performed with respect and dignity—can become our most fruitful yeses.

Our society's most readily identified heroes—members of the military, police officers, firefighters, and emergency medical workers—enter tough, often dangerous, work environments every day. They are lifesavers, and we all see that. But a farmworker's yes to a day spent in the hot sun harvesting fruit, a plumber's shift untangling a jammed pipe, or a dad's morning with cranky toddlers and too many diapers also have inherent worth and demand to be done with dignity. God created us for work, and our work can make us holy when we give ourselves to it with generous hearts and minds open to creativity.

To Ponder

1. When someone asks you about your work, how do you respond? Does your work or your career define who you are?

2. What do you love and how is your work—even remotely—related to that?

3. Does your prayer life shape the manner in which you do your work? In what ways?

4. Have you ever struggled with unemployment or underemployment? How was your generous giving of yourself in those circumstances a factor in the way you moved through that time?

5. How do you open yourself up to the potential for creativity in your work?

6. What is your standard for perfection in your work?

7. In what ways is your work a yes to God? What changes do you need to make in your work life to be more open to God's will for you?

Let us pray.

God, Creator of all,
thank you for the work you give me every day.
I praise you for a vocation that allows me
to glorify you daily
through the fruits of my labor.
Help me to perform my work for your glory,
to be more open to your will for my days,
and to sense the creativity you have instilled within me.
May my work be productive,
may it be offered for the benefit of the world around me
and never only in satisfaction of my own ego.
May my work always be worthy of the gifts
you have placed within me.
Amen.

4. The Grace *of* Integrity

I admit with no small degree of embarrassment to watching with a blend of amusement and horror as televangelist Jim Bakker and his then wife Tammy Faye Bakker lost their ministry, marriage, and reputations over sex and accounting scandals in the late 1980s. I also smirked at Jimmy Swaggart's very public confession of sin involving a prostitute. He too lost his ministry and public credibility right about that same time. I wondered how genuine their tears and remorse could possibly be. In 2001, and for too many years since, I have puzzled in disgusted amazement at the number of priests who have victimized innocent children in my own Roman Catholic Church. I tried not to judge, but I really could not grasp how these horrible actions came from men who promised their lives to leading others to God. One would think that religiosity and integrity would walk hand in hand. Not necessarily.

During the last ten years or so, I've come to the conclusion that people of faith, and especially those who of us who witness to our beliefs in the public arena, are constantly at risk of breaching the virtue of integrity. Because we endeavor to share the Good News in word and deed, we may sin by putting forward a false version of ourselves. Aware that others are watching us, we may act or speak in a manner that is inconsistent with the totality of our truest selves.

As I began developing CatholicMom.com as a ministry, I began to catch a small glimmer of comprehension about the circumstances that led those men with so much religious power to such depths of depravity. While I certainly in no way excused their sin, I began to understand the dangers of working in ministry, of always being on, of always forcing oneself to put on a public persona, and of interacting with loads of people who want from you more than you might have to give.

Some of you will giggle at my thoughts that flee to the old *Saturday Night Live* character Church Lady and her pious conviction of Satan as the dastardly force behind bad behavior. I wonder time and again, can the dark one really be the engineer of so many failings of integrity among religious leaders?

Living with the effects of the hectic pace and stress of my own work, I began to more easily see how someone could be preaching God's love by day and give in to sinful excesses by night. While my work hasn't led me to scandalous levels of sin, it has perhaps put me in more positions to make ethical compromises than had I not ventured down this road. This may sound like a bit of a cop-out. If we all are vulnerable to sin, how can ministry work make one more or less susceptible to infractions of integrity? I can only speak from my own experience, of course, but the role I've assumed as a Catholic media professional leads me both closer to God on a daily basis and closer to tripping into evil.

If I'm completely honest, integrity in my world is a daily decision, a virtue and skill that must be consistently honed through determined and conscious practice. And all too often, I falter. Doubt and despair, vanity and envy are all real factors in my life. I hold myself to high standards and others do as well. Often my frustration and disappointment with my failings leads me to make bad choices and to compromise my integrity.

I am often tempted to throw up my hands in despair when I fall short of the goodness of heart and the generosity of spirit I desire. When I am plagued by doubt or questions about the nature of the faith I profess, I work overtime to present a confident Lisa instead. Ironically, in my own effort to draw others into a closer relationship with Jesus Christ, not infrequently I neglect my own faith walk, especially when trying to remain honest about who I am.

The increased awareness in recent years of my vulnerability to sin has been a blessing. Like a yellow light that warns me to hit the brakes when I'm driving, the spiritual darkness I feel in near occasions of sin reminds me to slow down, to see the signs of a fall, and to seek solace in the arms of the One who is the source of all light and of unconditional love. In him, there is hope.

Am I My Avatar?

Working online, I've become very familiar with the cultural phenomenon known as an *avatar*. In the tech world, an avatar is an icon or figure representing a particular person. Avatars are used in gaming online and also in social networking, online forums, and blogging venues.

If you spend any time on the Internet, you know the significance of a good avatar. It's your "face" to those you interact with there. When I have the opportunity to meet an online contact in the non-cyber world, I'm always struck by the experience of her avatar coming to life, so to speak. Far from simply learning what they look like from the neck down, these "in real life" (or IRL) friends thereafter take on a 3-D quality in my mind that forever helps them escape the confines of a simple head shot.

If you've used an avatar, then you know some of the grief that can go into the process. You want a photo that looks like you but on a good hair day, with the right lighting, and, preferably—for many of us—a slightly slimmer, younger-looking version of our true selves. I look for an avatar that belies the fact that half the time I'm working in dirty gym clothes or my pajamas—both benefits of working from home but not the picture of professionalism I aim for.

My avatar's typically just had her hair done and she's calm, unworried about deadlines or work-related stress. My avatar never misses morning prayer time. You can tell by that peaceful, composed look in her picture that she begins her day with her priorities in place. My avatar doesn't binge on chocolate when she's stressed and is only an occasional social drinker. She doesn't consider chardonnay a food group. She's never donned her running shoes in the morning and worn them all day thinking she'll "get around to" fitting that walk in soon. My avatar doesn't check on things like stats about how well her books are selling on Amazon or how many people have "liked" her Facebook status. She is humble through and through. In other words, my avatar is often a fictitious character.

On my best days, my avatar represents some of the aspects of my life as I wish they were more consistently. A true avatar would more honestly picture me in sweat pants, rushing to beat a deadline, mumbling to myself about finding time to pray later while hoping that my wonderful, patient husband won't mind that the house could use a good cleaning and his belly could use a home-cooked meal.

The "integrity problem" kicks in when I begin to put forward the impression that I am my avatar. And, once again, I'll underscore that this can be a tremendous temptation for anyone, but perhaps especially for those of us who work in mission territory. And if our mission territory is online, the temptation is even greater. I won't speak for other faith-based bloggers, but I must say that I consistently pray for the courage to be real in my writing. As I age, I fear the trap of putting forth an online persona that is inconsistent with who I really am.

This is where a yes to integrity kicks in. In my personal and professional lives—which are closely intertwined—being a woman of integrity means sharing my heart and soul about the beliefs I espouse and hold dear. But it also means being upfront about the sin in my life,

the many ways in which I fall short of the standards I
hold for myself.

I am not my avatar. I am Lisa.

What version of yourself do you put forward as
your avatar, either in social media or in the "real" world?
Do you struggle, as I do, to create a fictitious version
while knowing inside that the truth is vastly different?
When we allow ourselves to do this, our integrity is
compromised, and we also squelch our generosity in
favor of allowing others to believe something that is
false.

Integrity Redefined

If I'm correct, others struggle with the same challenges
I face when it comes to living a life of integrity in a
technologically evolving world. When I was growing
up, cheating in school meant the act of copying off of
someone else's paper or having that person do your
homework for you. Effective cheating meant that you
either had to have both good eyesight and an unob-
servant teacher or a friend whose handwriting could
pass for your own. Fast-forward forty years, and today's
elementary-school students keyboard instead of hand-
write and face the very real temptation of Googling, not
only to help them find the answers they seek but also
to provide pre-written essays at the touch of a button.
Their adult counterparts fall prey to grown-up versions
of these very same temptations. How very simple it is
today to employ technology devised to aid us and to
end up chipping away at our integrity in the process.

On the one hand, we face a Big Brother environment where someone's literally almost always watching. The Nanny Cam is a real tool used to supervise not only the babysitter but also just about anyone who is out in public. I recently had occasion to tour the manufacturing plant of a large security company. In its control room, a camera operator seated before a panel of a hundred small monitors could see offices, parking lots, and storefronts around the world. In an instant, he zoomed in on one poor, unsuspecting guy taking a smoke break while our tour group sat thousands of miles away watching and laughing about the smoker needing a haircut.

In many ways, technology has promoted a more secure world by decreasing crime. But I wonder sometimes if it has also caused us to cloister our questionable behavior to moments when we know that no one is watching. Oprah Winfrey is quoted as saying, "Real integrity is doing the right thing, knowing that nobody's going to know whether you did it or not." Perhaps integrity in today's world is the inverse as well: "Real integrity is *not* doing the *wrong* thing, knowing that nobody's going to know whether you did it or not."

Along with simply not cheating, saying yes to integrity means turning our backs on society's new norms. It means living within our means when everyone around us is maxing out their credit cards in "play now, pay later" ambivalence to fiscal responsibility. It means obeying the rules that keep society functioning, such as not speeding, paying our taxes, and exercising our right to vote rather than simply complaining about our politicians.

Integrity means being the change we desire to see in the world around us. And that change begins in our hearts and in our homes. Some of you will commiserate with this mom's too-frequent use of the phrase, "Because I said so!" as an easy way out of acting with integrity. Too often my sons learned from my bad behavior rather than my good words. I told them to play nicely and then turned to a girlfriend at the playground to gossip about a mutual acquaintance. I said no to a new toy they wanted because it wasn't prudent financially and bought myself a pair of shoes instead. I asked if they'd said their bedtime prayers and then fell off into an exhausted stupor without pausing to give my own thanks to the Creator of us all.

The blessing of family and loved ones is that even in the midst of an ever-evolving world, and as such presenting us with new tests of our integrity, those closest to us keep us honest by holding us to a higher standard. In Greg, Eric, and Adam, I see the souls of people who deserve to be loved and served to the best of my capacity. I see the opportunity for a generous giving of myself that commits fully to being honorable and honest, more for what my loved ones will gain from my acts than for what they'll think of me. We are often most honest, most ourselves, with those closest to us.

If I doubt my personal integrity, I don't have to turn much farther than to the person sleeping on the pillow next to me for a checkup. Between Greg and the God who knows every hair on my head, there is not much room to hide. And a yes to a life lived with integrity is a yes to a life lived wide open.

Set Apart

Modern-day integrity sets us apart from a world that is often looking for a shortcut to personal gain. Living with integrity makes us weird, perhaps even more so if the foundational motivation for our integrity is to follow the example of Jesus Christ. Even in the Old Testament, we find Solomon extolling the virtue of integrity. Proverbs 19 opens with the advice: "Better to be poor and walk in integrity than rich and crooked in one's ways" (19:1). In a world that seems to value fame and fortune, that is countercultural.

Pope Francis recently won a social-media smack down with Miley Cyrus for *Time*'s Person of the Year. So a religious leader who has reached out to the world with the promise of reconciliation and peace was nearly upstaged by a pop-music star whose sexually suggestive dancing caught more attention than the continuing crisis in Darfur and other war-torn regions of the world.

Perhaps this misplacement of priorities points to a need for more generous living that must begin in our homes. This was underscored for me in a chat I had early on in this writing process with my young nephew, Evan. An elementary-school student who is a voracious reader and loves video gaming with his little brother Tyler, Evan is always a fun person to visit. He was listening in when I chatted with his mom, my sister Erin, about the premise for this book. I was amazed by his interest and obvious enthusiasm for the project until he shared with his brother, "Auntie Lisa's writing a new book! *The Grace of DS!*"

I didn't have the heart to correct my godson and tell him I wouldn't be writing a book about his favorite Nintendo game. But the moment stuck with me. How excited Evan was about a cool gaming system! And how boring Auntie Lisa would have seemed if she'd corrected him and pontificated on the value of our yes to God, a book that would explore the true joy in generously giving of ourselves to those around us.

Clearly, the way to share my passion for this topic is not to lecture but to be a living, breathing role model for those little boys. That interaction taught me that my yes to virtues like integrity needs to be delivered with infectious enthusiasm. I wonder if I am prepared to tell everyone I meet about the gift of a life lived open to God's will, one that bends over backward to give generously in mind, body, and spirit in just the same way that Evan desires to share gaming fun with his brother.

If we want to be truly effective in our evangelization efforts, we must first realize that we will have greater influence because of our actions. We must behave with integrity always, being true to the people God created us to be. At the very least, that means loving and serving all whom we meet.

Most of us will not spend our days cloistered from a society that so frequently runs counter to the notions we hold most dear. But giving ourselves generously and with integrity means being ready to bloom where we are planted and to not be choked out by thorns, withered by drought, or trampled underfoot as we reach for the light. We are called to live our yes in the world as we find it and to speak our yes to that waiting world. The grace of integrity can teach us how to do that.

Small Matters Are a Big Deal

Saint Luke wrote in his gospel, "The person who is trustworthy in very small matters is also trustworthy in great ones; and the person who is dishonest in very small matters is also dishonest in great ones" (16:10). I am trying to be more attentive to small matters in my life that fly in the face of my yes to integrity. There are many moments during any given day when I am tempted to compromise my values for a more expedient solution to my long-term goals: the white lie, the shortcut taken, the politically correct response that won't rock the boat, a well-intentioned moral compromise, or the self-interested choice.

Small matters? Most of them, yes. In the running of an apostolate, a business, a family, or a church, these kinds of choices often seem to engulf us. The waters we wade in become so murky at times that we don't even notice a small matter come and gone until we're through it, the deed has been done, and the moment of remorse has kicked in. What then? Throw up our hands, call it a lapse in judgment, and move along?

Perhaps we cannot allow ourselves to be paralyzed by our all-too-human shortcomings. But let's also train ourselves to stop in these moments, to recognize any momentary lack of integrity, to make amends if possible, and to seek reconciliation. When we begin to look at life from this small-matter perspective, the challenge can be overwhelming. But Proverbs 16:3 holds our key to making it work: "Entrust your works to the Lord, and your plans will succeed."

....

To Ponder

1. How do you try to live as a person of integrity?

2. Describe your online avatar or public persona. How does this measure up to the way you actually live?

3. Do you think that integrity has been redefined in recent decades? In what ways?

4. Are you out of step with mainstream society in your moral choices and decisions?

5. What are some of the everyday small matters that challenge your integrity?

6. How comfortable are you entrusting the things that cause you to stumble to God?

Let us pray.

Father God, to whom I devote my every act and deed,
form in me the courage to choose a life of integrity.
I so greatly desire to lead a life of honesty
and accountability,
yet far too often I fall short
of the standards I set for myself.
I am learning, Lord, that this is a burden
too great to carry on my own,
and that it is a weight under which I cannot falter.
I entrust my works, my choices, and my acts to you, Lord,
with full knowledge that in and through you
nothing is impossible.
Carry me along the right path,
the one that leads me home to you.
I am yours.
Amen.

5. The Grace *of* Humility

Some of my best friends teasingly refer to me as The Diva. I don't remember when this moniker took on a life of its own, but the phrase both amuses and bugs the hell out of me. My podcasting buddies, who have been along for the ride since the time my life as a blogger began to grow into a full-fledged international apostolate, like to bandy about the title. They knew me when an interview I did for an online radio show caught the eye of a well-established religious publisher, who soon afterward invited me to submit a book proposal.

While many of the circumstances surrounding that invitation are now just fuzzy memories, I do remember elation and also fear. I really had no clear idea everything this next step might bring for me. But a tiny part of me comprehended enough to recognize that the public part of my existence might begin to take on greatly expanded parameters. Saying yes to a book definitely changed things. Mostly, it brought great blessings, but it also brought new threats to my humility.

A book succeeds because of both good writing on an enticing subject and a vibrant promotional platform created and sustained by the author. Both factors usually carry near-equal weight. Creating a successful book is at times particularly ironic in the world of spiritual book publishing, where an author also needs a well-developed spiritual life. That is sometimes hard to sustain while tending to one's platform, which of course requires a good amount of self-promotion and living in the public eye.

The very best spiritual books are the ones that move us toward deeper relationship with God, because in them we catch the genuine voice of an author who is a fellow pilgrim, and in varied ways we connect to it. To reach this level of authenticity in writing involves a keen capacity for introspection and a willingness to mine the deep recesses of one's spirit that aren't typically laid bare for public consumption. As I try to improve my craft, I look to current-day spiritual writers whom I admire. In them I see wisdom, depth, and an interior life that burns deeply. Most are introverts, and they know how to be quiet.

Even with today's technology, which makes the mechanics of writing fairly easy, the task requires me to close out the world, breathe in deeply God's grace, draw close to what I believe is his will for my work, and only then set fingers to keyboard. Writing draws me to a place deep within that urges me to see even the tiniest flicker of the flame God has kindled within me. I always pray first for the ability to comprehend what the Author of my life desires of my work. Writing is withdrawal, a journey within.

But then, when the book is published, I must shift aside the world-quieting skills that helped me write and embrace other skills that help me engage in a rich flurry of promotional venues, blog tours, networking opportunities, and exposure. "It's part of the gig," I tell myself, but this all becomes a great breeding ground for a puffed-up sense of self. So I cling to the grace of humility and pray that God causes it to blossom in me.

Thinking of Me Less

A common definition of *humility* calls it "the quality or state of not thinking you are better than other people, the quality or state of being humble." But my favorite description of the word comes from C. S. Lewis in his classic work *Mere Christianity*: "True humility is not thinking less of yourself; it is thinking of yourself less."

Pondering Lewis's simple quote can help us see how to reconcile the legitimate need to promote something we have created with the desire to never be self-centered. Whether you are an author or a plumber, a lawyer or a farmer, it's likely that if you labor at something, you will need to be involved in advertising your work to others, in simply calling attention to what you have accomplished. It occurs to me time and time again that there are appropriate ways for people of faith to do this and still live generously.

First and foremost, we must be utterly convinced that the gifts we have to share with the world come from God. If we are seeking an example of humility in action, we need only to look at Mary, the mother of Jesus Christ, who gave all the glory to God when her cousin Elizabeth recognized the Savior of the world dwelling within Mary's womb. Her canticle in the first chapter of Luke's gospel is a song of true humility (see Lk 1:46–55).

Mary's yes to God's will for her life was a continual generous giving of herself to his will, even when it was most heartbreaking. In this particular moment of encounter with Elizabeth, Mary—unwed and pregnant—portrays the attitude I want to carry when my work circumstances require me to act in ways that feel anything but humble.

I try to bear a gift from God to my own small corner of the world. Because of Mary's example, I am more confident as I bring that gift forward in praise of our God.

Deepening the Foundation

True humility will not come naturally or easily for many of us. I've been praying of late for the ability to put The Diva to the side and let the child of God within me shine in her place. The Diva dodges compliments but expects special treatment. The Diva is terribly concerned with appearances and achievements. She doesn't always expect to be recognized, but she really loves it when she is. The Diva has a lot of friends but never enough true friendships. She would like others to believe that she is a humble person, but in reality she's got a long way to go before her actions and intentions are free of ulterior motives and could be called truly humble.

A large part of me is ready to let The Diva go by the wayside and in her place shine a light on who I am as child of God. The child of God isn't vain or self-centered when being true to herself. She marvels at the audacity of the sunrise and happily extols the majesty of the ocean. She clings to the life-affirming relationships she has and lets them surround her like a security blanket that keeps her safe and warm. The child of God whom I keep striving to be is ready and willing to glorify God in simple, precious ways and to praise him when the fruits of his work in her are pleasing to others.

Humility, like fame, rarely grows to full bloom overnight. Humble, generous giving of oneself to the work of God involves conscious choices and lots of practice. It requires building a solid bedrock of humility that can withstand the temptations of too much self-promotion. When humility collides in our lives with popularity or fame, perhaps we can find solace and clarity of vision in words attributed to Saint Augustine:

> Do you wish to be great? Then begin by being.
> Do you desire to construct a vast and lofty
> fabric? Think first about the foundations of
> humility. The higher your structure is to be,
> the deeper must be its foundation.

It is precisely a bedrock of humility that can keep our ego towers from tumbling when the heights we reach cause us to lose touch with our grounding. A weak foundation of humility might account for a pop-singer's drug addiction, a church leader's sex scandal, or an author's unwieldy egotism. When our popularity comes and its forty-story deluxe tower is built upon dust instead of the steel and concrete of humility, all it takes is the tiniest of winds to set the whole structure toppling. When that happens, our openness to God's will for our lives— those yeses we wanted to give—are morphed into our own agendas. Sometimes we're even shrewd enough to convince ourselves that God really wants for us the self-centered paths we've chosen. Lack of humility clouds our ability to discern, and our over-inflated egos and "What's in it for me?" attitudes drive our decisions.

Growing in the grace of humility means catching ourselves in moments or seasons of our lives when we've ventured off course or our towers have toppled. It is rarely, if ever, too late to course-correct. But reaching out and grasping humility in our faltering can be daunting. Next time you believe that you've screwed up badly, that you're too far gone for hope, catch yourself. A humble yes in those moments has us reaching for help from God, loved ones, and anyone else who is nearby. True humility accepts help when it is offered and asks for help even when the world seems to believe we have it all together.

Portraits of Humility

A beautiful portrait of humility was painted on a stretch of Copacabana Beach in Rio de Janeiro in July 2013 as three million young people gathered in silent prayer at World Youth Day. In their midst, in utter silence, a singer knelt before them, his back to the crowd as he positioned himself before a cross with a guitar slung around his shoulders. Then, Matt Maher sang on his knees, his guitar his only accompaniment, his song a love letter that gave voice to the millions who had assembled that night to worship. His gift that night was for the God who endowed him with amazing talent.

I've watched the video from that night of Maher's singing "Lord, I Need You" a dozen times, looking for some trace of the self-satisfaction that such a heady moment must surely have brought for an artist who has devoted his life's work to ministry. Vanity and puffed-up pride seemed absent within Maher, their places filled instead by a simplicity of purpose that gleamed with pure intention. In the video, Maher quietly strums a graceful rendition of a song that is an anthem to humility, to our unending need for God in our lives.

With Maher's song still playing in my mind, I heard him interviewed on the process of songwriting and particularly on the writing of "Lord, I Need You." He offered a great lesson in humility and in the grace of saying yes to the gifts God has given him.

> The process of writing the song is really our act of worship. And it becomes the opportunity with which God ministers most to us. And then when we go out and we start leading the song, it's like it's a confirmation of what was impressed upon us when we wrote it.[1]

Watching Maher, letting this song sink into my heart, drawing me closer to Christ, I am reminded to look at how God ministers to me in the work he has called me to do. I encourage you to do the same: to take those "Wow!" moments when the work you produce is compelling, beautiful, or simply awesome and see them as God's handiwork through you. When we see our work like this, we give glory to God with a yes in our hearts, and when we share his work in us with those we meet, we take a step forward in humility.

Present that night on the beach in Rio was another humble man. He wore white vestments and sat in silent prayer. Just a few months earlier, the man had given his "Yes, Lord" to become pope, Holy Father to a worldwide Church awaiting a new shepherd. The events leading up to the election of Pope Francis left many saddened by the decision of his predecessor, Pope Benedict XVI, to retire. In that choice, Pope Benedict also pointed the way to humble service, pushing a Church outside its comfort level with confidence that it was God, not himself, who would provide the worthy answer.

At the end of 2013, the new pope, whom so many had come to characterize as humble, was named *Time*'s Person of the Year. In a Vatican statement acknowledging the honor, Father Federico Lombardi explained:

> The decision didn't come as a surprise given the great resonance and attention surrounding the election of Pope Francis right from the start of the new pontificate. The fact that one of the most prestigious awards to be attributed by the international press should go to someone who promotes spiritual, religious, and moral values as well as call for peace and greater

justice in an incisive manner is a positive sign. As for the pope himself, he's not someone who seeks fame and success, because he has put his life at the service of announcing the Gospel of the love of God for mankind. It is pleasing to the pope that this service should appeal and give hope to women and men. And if this choice of Person of the Year should mean that many people have understood this message—at least implicitly—the pope is really happy about this.[2]

As we continue to watch the vision and mission of this humble spiritual shepherd unfold, it is becoming increasingly clear that the humility for which Pope Francis advocates is not a hidden, behind-the-scenes brand. Following Pope Francis's lead means leaving behind pretentious trappings while clinging to truth. And clinging to truth means discerning it, which involves prayer and practice. Humility challenges us to place the concerns of others before our own. But true humility also challenges us to be more, to be better, to be stronger for the world around us. Dying to self isn't enough if the space within us doesn't get filled up with living for others.

Humility and Forgiveness

I've been praying about and pondering the connection between humility and my ability to forgive. All too often my ability to generously give my full yes to God's will for my life is hindered by my own inability to forgive another or myself. So I took my wondering to the

members of one of my favorite philosophical salons—
my Facebook friends. We wrestled together with this tie
between humility and true forgiveness. Some of the most
insightful comments came from my friend Father Scott
Hurd, a published author on the topic of forgiveness.

Father Scott and other friends reminded me that
one thing frequently keeping us from truly forgiving
is our sometimes-misguided sense of justice. This is
especially true when someone who has wronged us
shows no remorse or sorrow. In those cases, I cling to
my anger as a self-righteous shield, assuring myself that
the grudge I bear is right and just, because *I* am right and
just. But Father Scott reminded me that true forgiveness
is an act of love and mercy, freely given and completely
without conditions or respect to one's worthiness.

By refusing to forgive, my yes is limited and my
own self-satisfaction is stoked. Holding on to a choking
anger is a temporary pleasure, like gorging on chocolate. But eventually we realize that while it tastes good
for a few fleeting moments, too much of the stuff over
an extended period of time will sicken both our bodies
and our spirits. The energy I give to *not* forgiving or
to holding a grudge is an unhealthy and often sinful
self-indulgence I permit myself. In my lack of humility,
I want to believe that I'm right. Meanwhile, a part of
my soul dies as my pride keeps me from accepting the
freedom offered by a God who forgives all, despite my
unworthiness.

Perhaps the most burdensome grudges we bear
are those we hold against ourselves when we refuse to
accept God's unconditional embrace. Just as our sense of
moral superiority may keep us from forgiving one who

has hurt us, or perhaps when one has injured a loved one of ours, we refuse to accept the limitless, boundless love God has for us. My friend Jennifer ministers to women who have had abortions and shared with me that this is a burden many of them bear. Even though a woman can accept intellectually that God forgives what she has done, she often places limits around God because she cannot accept that her sin is less than God's infinite capacity for mercy. There's a failure here, a struggle that so many of us share, to believe that God is more powerful than anything we can muster up.

My friend and fellow blogger Joanne McPortland gave perfect voice to this internal conflict that keeps me from giving a full and worthy yes to forgiveness:

> I think we sometimes confuse forgiveness and absolution. God forgives all sins except the refusal to accept his mercy. Contrition and a purpose of amendment are required for absolution, which is release from the guilt of sin. Jesus was not speaking in metaphors when he told the apostles to forgive not once, not twice, not seven times, but EVERY time—and nothing is said about waiting for an apology.

The hardest thing for me is getting past this notion of "deserving" forgiveness. I am much more willing to forgive others than to forgive myself, but that is no grace. Unwillingness to forgive, or rationing mercy based on the other person's (or one's own) level of worthiness, is human brokenness, not godlike action.

I have been the recipient of the grace of forgiveness in so many ways. The key way that I know this is a grace we are called to is that it is accompanied by joy so indescribable as to be only heavenly—both when we receive it and when we give it. Bearing a grudge, holding on to anger, or failing to ask for and accept forgiveness, on the other hand, feel like burrs under the saddle—ongoing, unrelieved irritation that colors the world and becomes the focus of everything.

It's very hard sometimes to truly accept forgiveness, as it is to truly forgive. Sometimes we hurt too much; sometimes we simply lack enough humility.

Faces of Forgiveness

In the fall of 2013, to mark the twentieth anniversary of the Rwandan Genocide, Catholic Relief Services (CRS) led a group of journalists to that country. We went to see post-genocidal developments and the good work CRS is doing there through peace-building initiatives. It's nearly impossible for me to reconcile in my mind, and certainly not in my heart, the atrocities of over half a million innocents slaughtered in the course of one hundred days in the spring of 1994. Most victims of the genocide were hacked to death by machetes in their own homes, neighborhoods, or churches. Many were killed by people they knew.

Ask me what I learned on this trip, and I can give you a substantial list of both facts and impressions, most of them horrific. Yet, near the top of my list is an increased amazement at the human capacity and desire to forgive. Throughout our time in Rwanda, time and time again, we met people whose lives were dismantled by the genocide. They survived enormous evil and yet found reason to hope.

We visited two national genocide memorials, at Kigali and at Murambi. Both memorials contain exposed bodies as well as artifacts owned by genocide victims. The Murambi Genocide Memorial Centre stands on the grounds of what was once the Murambi Technical School. In 1994, as tribal disputes in Rwanda grew into an insurmountable tide of killing, Tutsis from the nearby community were tricked into heading to the school atop a small hill. Rather than finding the shelter they expected, the college became a killing ground where more than 45,000 men, women, and children were massacred in the course of only a few days. Now a memorial site, Murambi exists to educate visitors to the horrors that unfolded there in the hopes that such evil will never again be perpetrated.

As a part of our visit to this place, we walked from the relative calm of the museum to the classroom buildings of that now-defunct school. In the rooms of one classroom wing, we followed our guide (himself a genocide survivor) through a series of classrooms where twenty-year-old desks were pushed together to form a resting place of sorts for hundreds of the men, women, and children killed in that place.

The memory of those bare, decomposing bodies is one I will never forget. From the skeletal remains, some with bits of flesh still withering to nothingness, emanated the stench of hatred and evil. I forced myself that day to walk among them, holding back sobs and the bile that rose from my gut, and to pray for the repose of their precious souls. They were men who gave their last breath to protect their families. They were women, a few with legs still spread wide, their bodies violated as their lives were taken. They were children and babies, too little to understand why their tiny bones were being hacked apart.

Our visit to Murambi was only a very small part of our excursion into the heart of Rwanda, but it was one that has left an indelible scar on me. In the months since that visit, I have endeavored to keep the memory of that terrible stench alive in my consciousness. I don't want to forget what I saw that day or how it made me feel. When I awake in a dank sweat after yet another violent nightmare where the sights and smells of Murambi return me to the space where I lingered among those innocent souls, I pray for the courage to not only remember their suffering but also to be a tiny part of ensuring that their legacy mandates change. Now, months later, I am still unable to speak effectively about the experience of visiting a place like Murambi without being driven to tears. I say this with humility, knowing how limited my insight into the situation truly is compared with the Rwandan families who lost so many loved ones and so much of their lives.

Standing in a room full of the corpses of young children gives you both a grief beyond understanding and a sense of conviction that each of us must rise up and act to avoid such unspeakable acts in the future. But how, in the wake of such despicable acts, is it possible to have any hope?

We met with a few groups of survivors. In Rugnago Parish in Huye, we held an intimate conversation with members of CRS's Community Healing and Reconciliation Program. One after the next, standing in pairs, a genocide survivor who had lost his or her family and livelihood during the genocide partnered with the person or a relative of the one who had done the killing, mutilating, stealing, or other horrific act. Time after time, these pairs told their stories. First, a perpetrator would rise and describe the crimes he or she had committed during the genocide. They described acts of theft, vandalism, physical battery, and even murder, often perpetrated on close neighbors and former friends who suddenly had become the enemy because of tribal warring. After these public declarations, the other person would rise and describe the ways in which he had been wronged, attacked, and left to live alone after the killing of his loved ones or the loss of their livelihood or property. And then, remarkably, he or she would turn and acknowledge the perpetrator directly next to him, extending a message of renewed forgiveness for all the things they had suffered, and often the exchange would end in an embrace between the two parties.

Perhaps the most memorable moment of the journey for me took place in a village atop a hill, amid one-room houses in a farm field. With the goats making noise in the background, widows of the genocide in Karmonyi rose one by one and shared their stories of survival and forgiveness. Among them was an elderly woman, Immaculee, who clearly had the respect of the rest of the group. As I approached to greet her, I noticed a broken plastic Rosary hanging around her neck. She grasped the beads as we prayed together, she in Kinyarwanda and I in tear-choked English.

While our languages kept us from comprehending each other's exact phraseology, I am confident that Immaculee saw into my heart that morning and understood. She knew that I could not possibly know the horrors she had lived. But she also comprehended that I knew God, and she smiled to tell her story. As we parted, I pulled from my backpack a favorite rosary, one blessed by Pope Benedict XVI. With tears, I passed those beads to their new owner, Immaculee, asking her to pray for my family and for my own ability to forgive.

When I catch myself bearing resentment or unable to forgive some wrong, I try to remember the people of Rwanda, survivors of genocide, and their still hard-to-believe determination to forgive—humbly and bravely.

To Ponder

1. What does true humility look like in you? Do you struggle with being humble? How so?

2. How does your daily work impact your humility?

3. What are some barriers that block you from thinking of others instead of yourself?

4. Name someone in your life who epitomizes humility. What are some of the traits that attract you to this person?

5. How is forgiveness tied to humility in your life?

6. Do you bear a wound that you are unable to forgive? Talk or write about it.

7. What keeps you from forgiving, even yourself?

8. How are humility and forgiveness intertwined with
   your ability to give God your yes?

Let us pray.

Jesus, I desire to be great in my love for you
and mighty in the fruit that my work can bear
bringing others closer to you.
But I falter under the weight of my own pride.
Egotism blocks me from serving others before myself.
False or lacking humility threatens my foundations.
Lord, from the Cross you taught us in word and deed
what love, humility, service, and forgiveness look like.
I desire to love as you did, humbly,
and with no hidden agenda.
I desire to forgive and to accept forgiveness,
at every turn and in all circumstances.
May my yes to your will for my life
be ever simple, humble, and complete.
In you, despite my frailties,
there is grace and hope.
Amen.

6. The Grace *of* Vulnerability

My ability to run any distance at a pace faster than a slow jog is nil. But my inner stamina and endurance are stronger than ever. My eyes are failing, and I'm hopeless without my glasses. But my vision for the future is clear and bright. I take medication to control my thyroid and blood pressure. But the capacity of my heart to love, and to be loved, feels boundless.

Coming to grips with the aging process is both an exercise in consenting to God's plan and an act of defiance. Some days, I am ready for the battle against the effects of fifty years of wear and tear. Other days, I'm prepared to throw in the towel and give in to the physical limitations I feel as I age. What's more and more apparent to me is that care of my physical body is increasingly important for me to worthily travel the path God has placed before me. But so is my ability to accept and to be realistic about my limitations. As I venture into the mystery of my fifties, I'm coming to some important realizations about the link between my physical body and my soul. Giving a full yes to God's will for my life means caring for myself so that both will stand up to the tests of this mission I'm on. But generosity of spirit also means living each day as if it were my last. Reconciling these two facts is an ongoing discovery of both my limitations and my vast potential.

Lessons from the Waiting Room

In the fall of 2013, I celebrated the fifth anniversary of my diagnosis with noninvasive breast cancer. I say "celebrated" intentionally, because for me that November discovery half a decade ago began a journey of understanding that continues to unfold for me.

My diagnosis was early and uncomplicated. Within a few weeks, I was headed into surgery for a procedure to remove the affected portion of my breast and some surrounding tissue. Today, five years later, I can look at my right breast and see a small scar and a slight indentation. I can also look at five tiny tattoos on my chest and sides that mark the "targets" for the seven weeks of radiation, which killed off the bad cells that might have been left behind after surgery.

Sometimes, the whole ordeal feels like a dream, until I go back and read some of what I wrote in my journals during those months. And then I remember the feelings that I had—fear but also resolution. While my diagnosis was never a huge cause for concern, as my cancer was highly treatable, it was an important reminder to keep my priorities straight. Sitting in the waiting room of a cancer center every day for seven weeks will do that to you.

I decided to treat the experience as a mission of sorts. I committed myself to attending daily Mass (not something I've ever been very faithful to despite my best intentions), and I asked friends for their intentions to pray over during my time on the radiation table. Interestingly, sometimes that list was longer than the few moments it took to receive my treatment. What a surprising grace it was for me to focus on the needs of others rather than on my own fears during those several weeks.

But on the very first day, I was petrified. And in my path, God placed a lovely woman who was just completing an important phase of her treatment. She had undergone chemo and as a result didn't have a single hair on her head. I remember the lovely scarf she wore, probably as much for warmth that cold January morning as for any cosmetic concern. I sat with her as I waited to be radiated, not knowing what that meant. She quietly shared her joy at the positive prognosis she'd just been given by her doctor. She cried with happiness for the extra months she'd been promised. I cried with anguish at the memories of friends I'd lost to the disease and at the reality of the challenge that lay before this woman.

We parted, promising to pray for one another. I'm sad now that I didn't ask her name, didn't know more about her life. But I have stayed true to my promise to pray, and I often thank her in my prayers for the message of hope she offered me that day. I like to imagine that she, too, celebrates being five years out. I like to pretend that her last five years have been filled with as many "Wow, God!" moments as mine have. She reminded me that morning that this life is a gift, so fragile and yet so overwhelmingly blessed that we can never take it for granted.

Another of my teachers at the cancer center was "José," a young boy who came onto the radiation table immediately after I was finished each day. The first week, his mother was with him, but in subsequent weeks paramedics who had brought him from the children's hospital wheeled him in on a stretcher. His mom, single and without much money, had to work to pay for his treatment. I never knew José's diagnosis, but his smile stays with me. Even in his sickness, his eyes lit up the waiting room. Perhaps José didn't understand fully the depths of his illness. With that smile and those eyes, from his prone position on that stretcher, he taught me to guard my joy and to let it shine, even when the chips are stacked against you.

Over time my visits to the cancer center have become less frequent. It's as if they wean you off of the place—if you're one of the lucky ones. They help you find your wings, guide you out of the nest, and teach you to fly off to whatever your future holds. After my regular treatments ended, I became one of the waiting-room people. Unlike those daily clients who slipped directly into the locker-room changing area to don gowns for treatment, the waiting-room people were at different phases of their care. Some of us were done and simply back for follow-up visits. Others were the newbies, newly diagnosed and coming for the very first time, filled with trepidation. But also among us were our companions, loved ones who came along to drive, to hold our hands, and to pray with and for us. And from them, too, I learned some important aspects of yes, of giving of myself generously while expecting nothing in return.

Watching the faces of my waiting-room companions, I learned the heart-wrenching pain of having to accept the illness of a loved one. I often watched parents in that waiting room and knew with certainty that most of them would—in an instant—take upon themselves the sickness of their child if they could. I also saw the opposite—children caring for their parents. From children of all ages, I learned the impact that being there for a loved one can have. Whether it's a shoulder to lean on (often literally), someone to ask the questions, be a second set of ears, or simply to sit quietly and pray for you while you face the test of a health-care challenge, the companion is a hero, called to a unique and excruciating yes of his or her own. From the companions, I learned both the pain and the potential of that particular yes. Both patients and their companions reminded me time and time again of the surprising grace of vulnerability, especially when we are forced to acknowledge the very real presence of death, which is never far from us.

Aging Gracefully

When I was younger, I looked at my parents and imagined what my life would be like at their age. As a schoolgirl, I admired their frequent date nights and the great parties they threw at our house. Looking back as the eldest of five, I can appreciate the fact that our perennial babysitter, Nancy, felt to me like a part of our family. How awesome it now seems that my parents prioritized their marriage enough to realize that they needed to spend time enjoying each other, at least sometimes without everyone else around.

In my college and newlywed years, as much as I loved my parents, they seemed so much older than me. I remember our party for their twenty-fifth wedding anniversary: Who could ever imagine being married that long?! On our twenty-seventh anniversary, just a short time ago, I recalled those feelings with a smile as I realized how in so many ways, Greg and I are still really just discovering one another. That must have been how my parents felt back then, when I was classifying them as dinosaurs. In that moment, my parents' vast span of time together was again a confirmation for me that age is a state of mind.

At the midway point of Eric's senior year in college, our extended family descended from far-flung points to visit him at Harvard. It was fun not only to share Eric's experience with my parents on their first campus visit but also to think back to my own time at Notre Dame and how recent those years felt in my heart. Anticipating our visit, I decided to rent a wheelchair for my mother. Mom doesn't use one normally and still gets around incredibly well, but I knew we would be doing a great deal of walking, and I wanted her to be comfortable. Ironically, about twelve hours into our trip my dad, who walks three miles every morning before working all day and ending his evening with nine quick holes of golf, hit a loose brick in a Boston sidewalk and landed in the hospital. Dad emerged eight hours later with five stitches in his forehead, his broken ankle in an air cast, and a haggard fifty-year-old daughter pushing him in the wheelchair we'd gotten just in case for Mom.

One sidewalk slip and an ER visit combined to help me realize that not only were my parents aging, but I was as well. Coming to this conclusion has helped me to pray about how my yes can extend and be refined into the years I have ahead of me. For years, I feared the vulnerability of the aging process. If I pondered getting old, my thought process was clouded with too many "What if?" worries and the perceived loss of dignity that must surely accompany aging. I realize now that for my yes to be continually valid as I grow older, I must be both gracefully aware of this vulnerability and allow myself to be susceptible to it.

I also want to claim the newfound pleasure that will come with mindfully greeting the changes as they come. Mentoring young writers who share their gifts on my website has given me a foretaste of this. No, I may not be the perfect person to recommend the latest in children's trends, but I can provide an opportunity and support for mothers learning to find their voice in their writing. The vulnerability of being out of date can be morphed into championing new voices and praying for their success as they take center stage.

I'm also reminded to look to mentors of my own and to increasingly hear and value their perspective. Admittedly, in the past, I was woefully disrespectful of the aged, and even at times of my own grandparents. Their limitations made them easy targets for teasing and, sometimes, even the butt of jokes at family gatherings. As my hair begins to gray, I feel the pain this must have caused them and recognize the loss I feel when I think about opportunities squandered. How wise they were. How much they had seen and experienced over the course of their lives! I wish my fifty-year-old self could go back to her thirty-five-year-old counterpart and tell that busy woman to spend more time lingering in their presence, actively listening to those old back-in-my-day stories with which they tried to teach me.

The vulnerabilities that accompany the aging process—the dimmed vision, weakened back, blurred memory, and small pains—now feel like a new and different "Yes, Lord" moment. I pray now for the grace to accept the rounded curves of flesh where once muscle sprouted, the lines on my face that mark the passing of the years. Don't get me wrong—I'm not giving in prematurely to a life of leisure. It's still a great part of my plan to continue to care for myself physically, to be strong enough to do whatever God asks of me. But I also intend to let this slowed-down version of me be a springboard, a vantage point for catching new views of the path ahead of me.

Fulton, the Superhero

An amazing blessing of my current role is the opportunity to field frequent prayer requests from folks in need of support. During the course of an average day, it's not unusual to be in contact with scores of friends and readers by e-mail, on Facebook, and on Twitter who are requesting prayers for particular intentions. At times,

I feel overwhelmed by the enormity of the need of so many—the health crises, the economic pains, the family breakdowns. Some days the list of people in pain seems endless.

I used to try to come to a resolution in each prayer-request situation, to find a way in which I could personally be of help to the one in need who was contacting me. Of course, from my desk a thousand miles away, there was little I could do to help a family whose grandma had just been hospitalized, or another whose lights and heat were being turned off in the deep of winter because they couldn't afford to pay a bill. I have learned to rely on God's goodness in these moments rather than try to muscle out a solution that I think might help. When I hand these burdens over to the Lord, I more fully acknowledge his love and sovereignty over all things. It is God who saves, which frees me from feeling the need to.

This doesn't mean that I stopped praying with and for friends or that I don't try to help when I can. But it does mean that I continue to learn the path of humility by shedding the weight of things I can't control. In doing this, I became more observant of the tiny miracles sprinkled in my path each day. One of the amazing things about having so many people ask you to pray with and for them is the vantage point it gives you to see God's bountiful handiwork.

One winter morning, I received an emergency call from the family of Cassandra, one of the writers at CatholicMom.com. Cassandra's husband and four-year-old son, Fulton, had been in an accident on the family's homestead and had sustained terrible burns.

With the little one burned on more than 43 percent of
his body, he and Cassandra were airlifted to Shriner's
Hospital Burn Unit in Galveston for trauma care. In the
meantime, along with many other friends, I'd put out an
immediate plea for prayers and support for the family.

Among the many contacts I had that day was a call
from a woman in Texas who had heard of the family's
need. She'd diverted her bus ride home to go immediately to the hospital, where she was waiting and praying
when Cassandra and Fulton arrived. She didn't know
me, and she didn't know them. She just felt the call to
be present for whatever they needed in that moment.

Hers was just one of the many moments of incredible generosity of spirit that I witnessed over the course
of the first year of Fulton's fight for recovery. Fulton's
family had to live through those first few touch-and-go
months and then through the subsequent adjustments
and pain. But surrounding them were also so many
prayer partners, both known and unknown to the child
and his family, who lifted them up, beseeching God for
healing and peace.

For me, little Fulton remains a champion of yes, a
role model for what it looks like to accept God's will for
our lives. While I can never suggest that the tragedy of
Fulton's accident was God's will, I have learned from
watching this young child that even in the midst of a
tremendous catastrophe, it is possible to rise up and to
witness to the strength and dignity that God has created
within each of us, and to respond with yes to his will
even in the midst of deep struggle.

When I see photos of Fulton, I marvel at the recovery he has made and ponder the enormity of the pain

his parents have had to endure. But Fulton's will be a lifetime of challenges. He will have to deal with the ensuing surgeries and procedures related to having been so badly burned, and he will also be called upon to deal with a society that looks at scars like his and shirks from them, as though they were contagious.

Fulton and his family now meet such interactions head-on. Cassandra has created burn cards. These full-color business cards show a before-and-after view of Fulton's face. The back side of the card explains in a child's voice what happened that day and why he bears the scars from his burns. But the cards also offer important prevention and first-aid information to help other families try to avoid such a tragedy in their own homes. Fulton gives out the cards himself, a young child turned teacher and advocate. Instead of crying when he is met with resistance or unkindness, Fulton gives of himself generously so that other children might be spared his plight.

When we look at a hero like Fulton, we should be attracted, not repulsed. Fulton's should be the face of courage, a model of strength. And while it's somewhat easy to look on the visage of an injured child and feel empathy, how often do we see the grown-up version of that same challenge and withdraw or look away? I cast the first stone at myself here, for not seeing in those who struggle with disabling injuries or other physical challenges whole persons who have stories to tell. I sometimes forget to see the face of Christ in them.

Fulton's mom, Cassandra, has taught me a lot about serving our Savior by facing up to such tremendous moments of agony. She's shown me the yes I'd like to perfect in my own life, the one that rises to whatever occasion comes up, even when it is horrific. Fulton's family has also taught me to see our Savior in those who are vulnerable. It no longer feels like enough to whisper a quiet prayer and avert my eyes when I meet them. I now find myself wanting to see Christ in their eyes and to whisper my love for him in the way I encounter them. This may be as simple as smiling broadly, opening a door, or offering a hand. These are small, insignificant gestures—baby steps toward having one iota of an understanding of Cassandra's yes, or Fulton's courage. But it's my start.

The Face We Deserve

I find myself dismayed by our society's denial of some aspects of the aging process. I'd be the first to agree that we should do all we can to countermand the physical impact of aging by remaining physically active. The sight of a woman in her seventies jogging in my neighborhood fills me with "You go, girl!" awe. I love the fact that my youngest brother and his wife have transformed themselves inside and out by their commitment to the CrossFit platform. My dear friend Mara is also my workout buddy, and I credit her with being my therapist as well as the one who gets me to the gym most regularly. But I am confounded by the seemingly unquenchable desire we have to drink from the cosmetic fountain of youth, to erase the lines that mark our faces and the gray that's sprinkled in our thinning hair.

George Orwell is quoted as having said, "At fifty, everyone has the face he deserves." While the writer didn't live to see fifty, this quip, like so much of what he wrote, comments on today's American society in prescient fashion. Before I cast too many aspersions, I'll fess up to the fact that without my hairdresser, my hairstyle of choice would be a salt-and-pepper-colored ponytail. I too have bought into the promise that we can retain a bit of what we had in the past with a few simple, chemical applications.

I find this increasingly frustrating and wonder if the pressure I feel to do something as seemingly innocent as coloring my hair limits the grace of my yes. How easily our desire to meet society's idea of beauty can turn into vanity and, worse yet, into a lack of love for ourselves just as God created us.

On the opposite side of this argument, I believe that presenting ourselves professionally coifed and clothed is important for our capacity to effectively convey our faith to others. When I stand before a crowd and share a presentation, I pay attention to the way I am clothed because I desire to be an effective messenger for God. I don't want my lack of care about how I look to distract from the Good News of the Gospel. Yet wasn't John the Baptist clothed in camel's cloak, his waist cinched with a belt of rough leather? Had he come in today's age, I wonder what he would be wearing.

So we work to balance care of our bodies with obsession over them. On my trip to Rwanda, I marveled at the simple beauty of the women I met. Those I encountered in farm fields or coffee plantations were free of the need to paint themselves with high-priced makeup or to sport the latest fashions. Their attire was conducive to the nature of their work, and yet it was their faces, their eyes, their hearts that struck me.

One of my favorite photos of myself from the trip is me at my most natural—eyes squinting in the sunshine, hair a mess, freckles aglow. When I look at that picture, I see my smile and I remember the joy I felt in that moment, how close I felt to God right where he had placed me that day. I'm happy for that snapshot, as it helps me to summon what "Yes, God" feels like on days when I feel exhausted and withdrawn, beaten down by a workload that feels insurmountable and wearied of falling short of the expectations I set for myself.

I'm fifty, and I have the face I deserve and the body that goes with it—the one God gave me. It's my responsibility to care for them, to guard them as best I can, and to recognize in them the changing tides that come with age and experience—and the grace of each vulnerable and courageous step along the way.

First, Do No Harm

As the wife of an emergency-medicine physician who is also a convert, I've often pondered the role that the Hippocratic Oath plays in my husband's life and the vocational choices he is called to make on a daily basis. I know his work environment and recognize that within his downtown ER's walls, he caters each week to hundreds of indigent families. Greg's care for his patients extends beyond their physical needs. He treats each patient with dignity, and his services are rendered without regard to a patient's ability to pay.

I often think about how generous the response of that structure is and how pure a physician's oath to "first, do no harm" should be. I believe that the vast majority of the medical professionals I know live by their oath, and I wonder if that same oath ought to extend to the rest of us.

A firm and conscious assent to God's will for our lives places on us the same responsibility to be unselfish in our caring for others and ourselves. For people of faith, a pro-life stance extends from womb to tomb. As such, we are called to care for those around us with dignity at every phase of life. To be consistently pro-life means to champion the rights of the most fragile: the child from the moment of his or her conception, the elderly confined within their homes or even their own minds, and the voiceless poor who may be unable to mentally or economically find their way through complex systems they need to survive. We are indeed called to be one another's keepers.

But how do we not crumble under the weight of so much human need? If we try to take it all in as individuals, it will feel insurmountable. But if we seek to approach human need together with other caring souls, the generous giving of ourselves has the potential for creating great change in our world. This involves living in the moment and heightening our senses to perceive the needs of those around us. If this overwhelms and frightens you, if you feel like it's too daunting a proposition to handle, then you are probably on the right track.

Since I'm not able to really comprehend the profound needs of so many, I try to begin with those God places most immediately in my path each day and to consistently ask these questions:

- Are the members of my family, including elderly relatives who live at some distance, safe, secure, and comfortable? Are their basic needs being taken care of? Am I doing what I can to share God's loving kindness with them?

- Do I help those in need in my neighborhood, city, and parish communities?

- Do I treat my physical body with dignity and respect? Do I take care of my psychological and spiritual well-being?

This last question may seem self-centered or arrogant. But if we are to "first, do no harm" in concentric circles of influence, doesn't this initially begin with not harming ourselves? Shouldn't a generous giving of ourselves begin with bodies that we respect and do not abuse with drugs, excessive alcohol, too much food, or illicit sex? If we come to our desire to please and to serve God from a position of brokenness in any of these areas, must not our path to reconciliation happen within a framework of self-healing?

But how hard this feels! How much easier it is to persist in our self-injuring ways, our drugs of choice. Because making true change means first and foremost admitting the harm that we do to ourselves and then beginning our baby steps along the highway to wholeness. For those of us who have given in to self-harm of any kind, the ability to seek healing is not found in a vacuum. We must bring ourselves to not only whisper our issues in our souls but also to speak them aloud to the God who knows all. Our prayers to do his will in our lives must include the petition that we be made strong enough to face our own demons, whatever they are. Then we must take the truly challenging step of finding help where it is needed. Self-care is also at the heart of being pro-life.

Living Through the Loss

Pain is real and stories of loss seem to enshroud us every day of the week. It's hard to reconcile the horrific trage-dies that occur in this world with the love of an all-pow-erful God. Whether loss stems from destruction brought on by human activity or from natural devastation, great loss gives us pause, shakes us up.

We asked why when a typhoon killed five thou-sand in the Philippines and begged to understand how a young man could stroll into an elementary school, open fire, and kill so many innocents. We wonder how and to what end bombs exploded, killing and maim-ing so many at the Boston Marathon in 2013. When the answers don't come easily, we might be tempted to sink into despair. Ironically, if you're like me and watched the news through those horrific stories, it wasn't hard to also see the valor of some who gave themselves most generously to God and to those in need. As much as we hate the moments of pain and grief, we are drawn to the images of unselfish love for one's neighbor. They motivate us to be a part of a solution, even if only in some small, modest way. We mourn, even as we get busy binding up and comforting, and Isaiah's song of prophecy becomes our mission in moments of pain so devastating we don't know where to turn.

> The spirit of the Lord God is upon me,
> because the Lord has anointed me;
> He has sent me to bring good news to the
> afflicted,
> to bind up the brokenhearted,
> To proclaim liberty to the captives,
> release to the prisoners,
> To announce a year of favor from the Lord
> and a day of vindication by our God;
> To comfort all who mourn;
> to place on those who mourn in Zion
> a diadem instead of ashes,
> To give them oil of gladness instead of
> mourning,
> a glorious mantle instead of a faint spirit
> (Is 61:1–3).

When the loss is closest to us, the pain can feel insurmountable. Following the death of a loved one, it's so tempting to cloister ourselves. We want to shut out the world around us and be solitary in our grief. In these times, perhaps we forget that those around us desire to be of help to us. In doing so, they find their own grief healed or lessened. And in those times, our acceptance of love, care, and company is an act of generosity, too. In allowing ourselves to be cherished and resuscitated, we give as much as we receive.

....

To Ponder

1. With what health-care challenges have you or a loved one struggled?

2. What did these situations teach you about your yes to God's plan for your life and your ability to accept limitations generously?

3. How do you feel about the prospect of aging?

4. Name your own yes superhero, a person who has had to face serious obstacles in his or her life. What have you learned from this person?

5. Describe your face—what do you love about yourself as God made you? Do you wish you were different somehow? Why or why not?

6. Do you or a loved one struggle with self-harm of any kind? What plans can you make to seek healing and relief?

7. What loss have you experienced in your life? How have you been open to generously receiving God's love through the aid of others around you?

Let us pray.

God, comforter, source of all solace,
be with me in my moments of brokenness.
I thank you for the gift of my physical body
and the presence of your Spirit within me.
Strengthen me physically to do your work
in a world so greatly in need.

Embolden me with a passion to care
for the minds and bodies of your people.
Give me courage to reach for help when I need it
and grace to see the needs of those around me.
As my body, my spirit, and my soul are your gifts,
may they be used to do your will.
Amen.

7. The Grace *of* No

My life's work is due in small part to a no I said when our son Eric was in early elementary school. As part of our commitment to the school, we parents were required to perform at least twenty volunteer hours per year. Most of us did far more, and I learned early on that all volunteer hours are not created equal. During Eric's kindergarten year, I found myself on a school auction committee with a wonderful group of fellow kindergarten parents. While our time together seeking auction donations helped me to gain a new group of friends, I realized early in the process that I was out of my element.

We were successful, but the work confirmed for me something I'd long suspected: I *hate* anything to do with fundraising. I like to tease my mother that this stems back to my Camp Fire Girl days when we had to stand on the sidewalk in front of a local bank on Friday afternoons peddling cans of Almond Roca for a troop fundraiser. I hated every minute of it.

After a very short time with the auction committee at Eric's school, I realized that this was not the volunteer job for me. I spent time considering the alternatives, and when a school newsletter advertised for a volunteer to implement a new website, I marched into the principal's office and signed up. That no to a committee assignment that didn't suit me turned into a yes that became the doorway to my life's work, because by overseeing the school's website for ten years, I learned a lot about technology and began to see the potential of connecting with others online. In a more immediate blessing, my work at the school taught me the needs of the organization and helped me build tremendous relationships with our administration, faculty, and school families. My no to fundraising and yes to the website opened doors that allowed me to make an enduring commitment to both our school and my parish, where I still serve as webmaster.

Why Say No?

It may appear a contradiction to have a chapter by this title in a book all about saying yes to God's will in our lives. Setting limits may seem to fly in the face of my advocacy for erring on the side of generosity. But the more I live in a yes mind-set, the more I realize the mandatory presence of a few, well-timed no responses along the way. Far from being a contradiction, a well-discerned negative seems to be a survival skill when you begin to live the grace of yes. I liken this to a lottery winner in his new millionaire status who is advised to seek legal representation and to go into seclusion upon hearing the big news of his newfound wealth. When others hear of his good fortune, they are going to want a piece of the action. And share he should, but not prior to discerning the best possible course of action and setting priorities. Only then can he be a good steward of the blessings of his newfound wealth.

For some of us, saying no is far more challenging than diving into a new opportunity and figuring out the details later. Saying no requires more forethought, more discipline, and also a kindness that may seem contradictory to realizing and accepting our limitations. A kind and well-intentioned no is a necessary part of the bedrock of a life devoted to giving God our full and worthy yes.

To this day, I do not enjoy asking people for money, for help, or even for prayer. I would rather be on the giving end. Ironically, I've come to see that what I thought was self-sufficiency is actually more of a partially veiled vanity. My pride keeps me from wanting to reveal that I may not have my act together. But learning the genuine joy of giving has helped me to be more generous in allowing others the same blessing I feel when I can be generous. I am learning to let others help me.

No and Not Knowing

That tiny no moment of mine at our boys' elementary school pales in comparison to the choices some of my friends have been called to make in their lives. My friend Steve is a shining role model for me in the way he has remained open to God's will. Steve's generosity of spirit took him half a world away a few years ago when he accepted a position as a lay volunteer teacher at a small seminary in Papua New Guinea (PNG).

Accepting this missionary role was a genuine leap of faith. Steve said good-bye to a good job and a home he'd known for years to embark on a journey into the unknown. Volumes could be written detailing all the little factors that played into his yes, but at the heart of it is Steve's ongoing willingness to see God's plan for his life and to do God's will. His trouble-laden travels to PNG took nearly five days. When he finally arrived, he withstood difficult adjustments to the language, the living conditions, and his new students. Through it all, he did his best to share the experience with those of us who were praying for him and watching it all unfold on Facebook and at his blog from half a world away.

Midway through Steve's time of commitment, an accident within his family called for a sudden change in his plans. For years, Steve had served as the primary caretaker of an elderly relative, who had a sudden and serious accident. Steve was needed back home immediately. My friend prayed about what walking away from the seminary where he was teaching would mean to his students, his fellow teachers, and the commitment he'd made.

Eight thousand miles away, I began to struggle as I tried to understand what my role should be in this situation. I had spent a great amount of time in discernment before deciding to go to PNG. It had been a tough decision, but one that I clearly felt I was being called to. Suddenly, I was faced with a new situation at home that had me wondering if I should return home only eight months into my commitment.

When Steve was finalizing his discernment to return home to his family commitment, he shared Thomas Merton's "A Prayer of Unknowing" on his blog.

My Lord God,

I have no idea where I am going. I do not see the road ahead of me. I cannot know for certain where it will end. Nor do I really know myself, and the fact that I think I am following your will does not mean that I am actually doing so.

But I believe that the desire to please you does in fact please you. And I hope I have that desire in all that I am doing. I hope that I will never do anything apart from that desire. And I know that, if I do this, you will lead me by the right road, though I may know nothing about it.

Therefore I will trust you always; though I may seem to be lost and in the shadow of death, I will not fear, for you are ever with

> me, and you will never leave me to face my
> perils alone.

In the end, after great discernment, my friend's no to one mission simply became an open door to a newly defined yes in his life and to a path that is still unfolding, still not completely clear. Sometimes, the ability to change our plans midstream—especially after they've come as a result of extended prayer and discernment—can leave us questioning exactly who is in charge of our lives. If we're wise, like Steve was, the answer is in our hearts, waiting to be discovered.

Affluenza and the Setting of Limits

As a mom, some of the most heart-wrenching nos I've had to say were to my sons. Every parent deeply desires to give his or her children the very best. At times, this means giving nothing, setting limits, calling a time-out, or outright saying, "No way!"

The term *affluenza* has recently come into the popular lexicon. Like *selfie* or *twerk*, the made-up word points to the societal context into which it was born. A combination of the words *affluence* and *influenza*, the term denotes "a painful, contagious, socially transmitted condition of overload, debt, anxiety, and waste resulting from the dogged pursuit of more."[3] In late 2013 the condition was actually successfully used as part of a legal defense when a teenager was acquitted of drunk driving. His excuse: affluenza, brought on by non-limit-setting parents who he contends had raised him to believe that wealth exempted one from consequences.

The day the affluenza verdict was announced, I sat and asked myself if I'd said no to my children enough. Had I enforced rules, set reasonable limits, and held them to a high enough standard of conduct? I'll be the first to admit what a challenge this is. We love our children, and all too often we believe that love is the equivalent of giving. There are plenty of times when I have masked my busyness with gifts of material goods or caved in when my maternal instincts demanded a stronger line be drawn in the sand.

Raising Eric and Adam to know and to respect spiritual and societal covenants has helped me put into greater context God's commandments for me. Just as a mother says, "In our family, we don't . . . ," we Christians abide by a code of expectations. Just as we parents know the benefits of sometimes denying the allure of immediate gratification or of not spoiling our loved ones, God knows the same for us. He teaches us the grace of no out of an abundance of compassion and concern. In the heat of the moment, the standards to which we Christians are held may seem unfair. Like a petulant toddler, we stamp our feet, pout, and whine (or growl), "But everyone else is doing it!"

Ever our benevolent parent, God the Father sets benevolent limits in the context of scripturally inspired commandments. In my broken state, I love to prayerfully ponder various reflections upon the commandments as I prepare myself for the grace of confession and reconciliation. The legalist in me lets herself off easily: "I haven't killed, committed adultery, or stolen this week, Lord," I pray in my rationalizing. While perhaps

I haven't broken the letter of the law, rare is the week when I haven't smashed its spirit to smithereens.

There are those limits again, calling me to a higher standard of self-giving generosity. My no to committing adultery calls me not only to not physically cheat on my husband but also to give myself more fully to the bond of our marriage vows. My no to coveting my neighbor's goods challenges me to live more simply, less materialistically, and with an eye toward sharing my gifts rather than acquiring in excess.

Greg and I set limits for our sons in their childhood and teenage years to keep them safe and to help them to thrive. We told the boys that the hours they spent studying instead of playing would pay off; that even though "everyone else" was doing something, they were expected to be different. We counterbalanced the rules we had in our home with generous love and encouragement, with hope for a future that would be bright and filled with promise. We followed the biblical tradition of Christianity, setting limits much as we find in the Ten Commandments and balancing those with a vision of a beautiful life promised to the upright, much as Jesus offers in my favorite gospel passage, Matthew 5:3–12, the Sermon on the Mount.

The beatitudes laid out in that passage are our source of encouragement when we rail against the persecution we face from a society that throws off behavioral limits as archaic. Like the commandments that came before them, the Beatitudes are a love letter, an encouragement, an assurance that the temporary challenges we face as disciples of the One who is all love will lead us to a bounty beyond our simple understanding. Inherent in both the Ten Commandments and the Beatitudes is a code for a life lived fully open to God's will, a generosity of giving that will never be fully unveiled to our complete comprehension.

So Heavenly Minded

My friend Marlene shared a saying in our couples' Bible study that's become a favorite of mine. Speaking of a church lady she knew who was on every committee and at the helm of every project, Marlene said, "She's so heavenly minded that she's no earthly good."

We know her, don't we? She's the first to volunteer to head up the potluck, yet her family's eating Happy Meals in the back of her van in the church parking lot. She's selling the raffle tickets to buy a new gadget the parish can't live without, but her checkbook's a mess and her bank account is overdrawn. She spends six nights a week at ministry meetings while her kids are being raised by electronic babysitters.

She's us, right? Many of us get so caught up in the good stuff we commit to that we make compromises requiring not only our own sacrifices but also those of our loved ones. Often the latter is expected or imposed without our loved ones' input or assent. It's easy for our desire to live generously to get confused with both our pride and our lack of discernment. Sometimes we're so heavenly minded about helping with the holy stuff we think is crucial that we're no earthly good to the people who need us most and to whom we are first responsible.

So does this mean that I stop giving of myself to worthy causes and needs beyond my family or loved ones? Absolutely not. It simply means that I must exercise some discipline and discernment before I jump into things. In these fresh empty-nest years, I'm still learning to balance the instinct to stay busy and distracted with the very real need to nurture my marriage as Greg and I enter a new phase of our lives together.

A recent conversation with friends showed me that many of us are challenged by this struggle to say no and keep our lives balanced. One friend shared her pastor's advice to listen to that small voice in your gut that's telling you to slow down when you're asked to be involved with a project or committee. He advised his congregation that the feeling of malaise we get, the sense that we need to take a step back, may be God's way of calling us to more prayer over the situation. When we skip the discernment and jump in headlong because we fear saying no, we may be walking away from God's plan for us, missing an important yes.

I'm trying to learn to listen to that feeling of malaise, to discern when it's born of God or born of my own agenda. Part of what makes a no grace-filled for me these days is taking time. This means rendering an assertive response when presented with an issue that requires discernment and forethought. Whether a request or invitation to share involves my time, our money, or my skills, I need to be humble enough to share with the source of the invitation that I need to pray and discuss before responding. I first need to slow down and ask myself at least three crucial questions:

- **How will this situation touch my soul?** Is this an opportunity to serve God by serving others, or will

I be saying yes primarily to serve my ego or to avoid looking bad? By engaging in this project, will I have an opportunity to grow in faith or to learn about my faith? By consenting to it, will I have the opportunity to share my faith with others or to be a light of Christ to someone else who may not yet know or love God? Will saying yes mean an impact upon my time that will keep me from daily prayer, weekly worship or spiritual reading and development? Does this invitation carry me closer to my ultimate goal in life—eternity spent in God's loving embrace in the company of my loved ones?

- **How does this situation impact my primary vocation as wife and mother?** Have I consulted with Greg about this invitation? Have we had a good conversation about what this means for our marriage and family, how it will impact our day-to-day routine and our future together? Will saying yes to this opportunity take me away from my home too much or cause me frustration that will later be vented upon my loved ones? If there is a financial commitment involved, will it be a strain to our family finances? Will my sons be blessed by my example of faithfulness and giving if I choose to accept this invitation?

- **How does this situation impact upon other commitments I've already made?** Will saying yes to this situation mean that I give less quality to my work or to other projects with which I'm already involved? Will a yes to this invitation be a blessing to my ministry or a distraction from it? Will it create connections that will be beneficial in the future? In saying yes will I lessen my efficacy or will I grow in a skill or knowledge that will serve those I aim to help with my work?

If I were smart, I would have a checklist with all of the above boldly and prominently displayed in my office and a laminated version in my purse for a handy reference. I would greet every invitation, offer, or solicitation with a kind, well-thought-out version of, "Let me get back to you on that." I'd learn from the times I acted in haste, convinced that my yes was both mandatory and well-intentioned, and the results were disastrous or detrimental. I wish I could say I had a spotlessly perfect record with the grace of no. But I'd be lying.

Luckily for me, I am an optimist who believes that old dogs can learn new tricks. One of my friends recently commented to me on this topic, noting that we need to dwell upon the kindness of no from both sides of the equation. On the delivery end, we need to take time when we respond no to something so that we do so with care and compassion. On the receiving end, we need to remember to accept a negative response to something we ask for with a kind and empathetic attitude. In both situations, we reflect the God we love and share with those around us. In these moments, our actions, motives, and words can either draw others closer to God or drive them from him, perhaps even permanently.

A few years ago, I was contacted by someone I'd known fairly well in the past. My interactions with this person left me knowing that she suffered from an addictive personality and was consistently deceptive. I learned about these traits the hard way—and personally—and didn't easily forget the hurt involved in our relationship. With prayer and time, I was able to come to peace and forgiveness, and also to a decision that the best reconciliation meant that I must limit my interaction with the person. This was easy, as our paths did not frequently cross in day-to-day life.

But one afternoon, the person contacted me and asked for monetary help. At the end of her rope, she had few other places to turn. The person knew me to be a Christian and also likely someone who had a hard time saying no. When the plea for help came, I wasn't surprised. But I also knew that a simple gift of money, no strings attached, likely wasn't the best solution to this person's problems. After prayer, I determined a course of action that involved sharing several good referrals and resources but ultimately not giving financial help. I carried the burden on my own without involving Greg because to have done so would have burdened him and infringed greatly on the privacy of this person.

But God heard from me quite a lot on the topic. In the days before and for a few weeks after the situation played out, my prayers were filled with concern and remorse. Had I made the right decision in saying no or simply the most expedient one? Enough time has since passed that I've found a sense of peace with the situation. What helped me with that was the knowledge that I had not simply refused to be involved but that I'd seriously tried to help in a way that was safe and resourceful. That no was given only after time, after prayer, and with the greatest amount of kindness and compassion I could muster given my history with the person in question. Was it easy? Hardly. But it was a step closer to understanding why no is at times not only prudent but also faithful.

Saying No to Ourselves

Sometimes the most challenging no we will say is the one we say to ourselves. Ask anyone who's ever tried to go on a diet, and you'll get confirmation of the cruelty of those voices inside our heads when we are trying to change a behavior or limit ourselves in some way. We may be able to muster compassion or concern for a loved one facing an extreme challenge, but place ourselves in that same position of fragility and we cut ourselves very little slack.

If you are someone who has never struggled with self-doubt, moderation, or ego, I invite you to skip the rest of this chapter and move along. But if, like me, you reserve your most vitriolic vocabulary for yourself, let's talk for just a few moments about why we do this and what impact it has on our spirit. Choose your dilemma—the thing that causes you the most sin and self-flagellation. How many times have you struggled with this problem and begged God for the strength to overcome it? How many times has your struggle been reprieved for a period of time only to be met with failure and even more virulent frustration?

Why does this happen? Why even in a prayerful state do we fall prey to our sinful nature? I think we get a small insight into the answer when we continue reading after the Sermon on the Mount, in Matthew 5:37, where we hear Jesus say to his followers, "Let your yes mean yes, and your no mean no. Anything more is from the evil one."

Perfection is not a state we'll experience in this lifetime. Your struggles with sin—the no you can't effectively say to yourself—may differ from mine. But most of us deal with something that is from the evil one. We can let our shortcomings and sin drive us into a pit of despair, or we can resolve to grasp for God's grace—so generously showered upon us—at every turn, one day at a time.

A friend who is familiar with the methodology and philosophy of Twelve Step recovery groups recently shared with me that they employ the saying, "Say what you mean. Mean what you say. But don't say it mean." While I've never attended a Twelve Step group such as Alcoholics Anonymous, my interactions with a loved one who is in recovery have led me to study the steps and to ponder them in relation to my own life. They are a powerful opening of ourselves to God's will, a yes with the power to render ourselves strong and to seek healing in light of the struggles over which we are powerless.

Steps four through seven help me to put into context this struggle I have with self-degrading tendencies. Those who have worked through these steps declare that they:

- made a searching and fearless moral inventory of themselves

- have admitted to God, to themselves, and to another human being the exact nature of their wrongs

- were entirely ready to have God remove all these defects of character
- humbly asked God to remove their shortcomings

We may not look at our sins as addictions, but the grace in these steps to say no to our defects but to not say it mean, and to look lovingly and humbly for God's intercession in our moments of need and grief, is a start along whatever path of healing we seek. If you struggle with this in any way, please remember that you are God's precious child.

Imagine holding your own child or a beloved little one in your arms as that baby lies limp and frail, injured and broken. Think for a moment about the pain that little one experiences and how you would lovingly take it from her in the blink of an eye to shield her from hurting. Then imagine that our God, who loves us so greatly, wants to do the very same for us. But first, we must humble ourselves to rest in his embrace. We must cast our cares upon him and have trust and patience as he begins to create wholeness and healing within us.

Self-hatred and a refusal to even begin to ask for help are from that evil one, the one who wants our yes and our giving of ourselves to be fragile or nonexistent. In order to fully live out the grace of yes in our lives, we must eliminate sources of defeat and weakness, things that render us powerless. If we can begin to see these choices as less of a no to a substance or behavior and more of a generous giving of ourselves to God's will for our lives, we take a step (or twelve) closer along the path that leads us home to him.

....

To Ponder

1. Do you have a difficult time saying no to people who ask for your help?

2. Why is this a challenge for you?

3. Have you had to face a decision in your life that caused you to change plans you had in place? How did that course correction impact you spiritually?

4. Do you find limit-setting to be difficult? What has helped you to set firm limits for your children or in your own life?

5. What factors do you consider when you are asked to help with a project or to assist someone?

6. What is the most challenging no you've ever had to say? How did this decision help you grow closer to God?

7. In your own self-inventory, over what behavior, substance, or choice are you powerless? How have you gone to God and humbly asked him to help you with this challenge?

Let us pray.

God, you are boundless and without limit.
I am weak, small, and unworthy,
yet filled with desire to be one with you.
So great is my love for you
that I desire to be your hands and your heart
to the world around me.

And yet in my humility, I fall so very short
of being and doing all that I desire.
Help me, Lord.
I come to you and humbly ask
that you perfect my flaws.
I beg your grace to understand my role,
and your wisdom to discern the choices before me.
May my yes mean yes and my no mean no,
today and always.
Amen.

8. The Grace *of* Rebirth

A friend of mine, someone I've known for more than a decade, walked away from practicing our shared Catholic faith a few years ago. I won't go into what caused my friend's decision, but the reasons were many and, some would say, largely valid. I noticed my friend's departure when it occurred, but I couldn't summon the intestinal fortitude to rock the boat and challenge his choice. "It's his prerogative," I told myself. "He's a good person, regardless of his religious practices." And that is true, but if I'm being honest here I must share that I knew there was pain and real grief that accompanied his decision. I was sure he knew the consequences of his choice not only for himself but also for his loved ones. I stood by, witnessed my friend's decision and the subsequent spiritual loss he surely felt, and did nothing.

Recent events had my friend thinking of a return to going to church. He trusted me enough to open his heart to me and ask for advice. And advice I gave! "Find the right church home." "Develop a relationship with a good spiritual director." "Read books *abc* and *xyz*, and anything you can get your hands on by so-and-so." I had all the right words to let my friend know that he was welcomed—that Jesus Christ and his Church wanted him home. But I didn't realize until I was at Mass the next morning that my yes moment with this friend had probably been squandered.

I sat alone in the pew at church that Sunday morning, listening as my husband and sons played the perfect liturgical music. My heart soared as my pastor gave a homily that seemed to inspire everyone. Then I noted the empty space in the pew next to me and I began to cry. Maybe that was my friend's seat—destined for him even if only for that morning. And it was empty.

Had I neglected to take the one step my loved one may have needed most? Should I have invited him to come to church with me that morning? How easy it should have been in the midst of the conversation we'd had the night before for me to say, "Come with me. I'll pick you up at nine. We'll have coffee after." I was afraid to press him too hard, to make him feel any discomfort. But in bending over backward to not crowd my friend spiritually, I'd abandoned him in a moment that could have resulted in his rebirth. As our parish family prayed together in my warm, cozy church that morning, my tears flowed for the opportunity I had wasted. I cried for having neglected to offer companionship, suspecting in hindsight that was what he may have needed most.

I prayed that morning for my friend and for myself. I prayed that we would both be born again—him by way of coming back to church and me by way of learning an ever-deeper yes to God's will not only in my own life but in the world around me as well. It's a daunting task, this yes to God. How easy it can be to give God the bare minimum of what he asks of me when I know full well the radical revolution to which I'm truly being called. I can give a million reasons why the time isn't right for my total rebirth. Yet I know the measure to which I am called is never greater than the resources God has given me to go all-in.

As weak as I am, God who is mighty and all-powerful has begun a good work in me. My effort to be a generous spirit is rooted in my desire to cooperate with every dream, every vision, and every deed God has in mind for me. Such cooperation often means getting my head out of God's way. If I overthink things, I can talk myself out of just about anything. If I neglect prayer, I lose my way. Much of what has come together in my life, especially in recent years, still confounds me. But when I look back and see God's presence at all the key junctures of my life, the road map becomes much clearer. Just as Jesus taught his disciples when they questioned in astonishment how any man could possibly be saved, I am convinced that for God, all things are possible (Mt 19:26).

Along my largely consistent believer's path, I have known desert times when I have thirsted for God's mercy and sunrise moments when a piercing clarity suddenly shone through the darkness, reassuring me of God's unending companionship. I love speaking with friends who have been born-again—who through merit of accepting Jesus Christ as their personal savior have undergone major transformation spiritually, which then spread to the other corners of their lives. As a lifelong believer, I can't imagine what such a vivid transition feels like, but I remain intrigued.

What does rebirth look like? Your answer to that will vary from mine. It's a tough concept to pinpoint, but I'm trying to train myself to recognize the potential for rebirth when it presents itself. I try to catch the potential in others and lend my support to the seedlings of hope I see in someone who is opening his or her heart and soul to a new life in God. And I try to catch the potential for rebirth in me and remain open to the small promptings that mark my own movements toward renewal.

Rebirth Done Right

As a writer, I'm always on the lookout for stories that will uplift and inspire, and I choose not to write about most negative stories. Call me Pollyanna, but I believe in the power of positivity to have an impact through the law of attraction. I believe that each of us can be the change we desire to see in this world. I could—and maybe someday will—write an entire tome on organizations, individuals, and entities whose generous giving of themselves leads others around them to rebirth. But for lack of space, I'll simply share a few of my favorite examples here.

His Chase Foundation was founded in 2010 in response to one couple's late-term miscarriage. In honor of their son Chase, who perished at thirty-five weeks' gestation, Mark and Chelsea Jacobs turned their loss and grief into fuel for a yes that now brings hope and needed resources to at-risk orphans in Ghana, half a world away. Empowered by the words of Isaiah 58, the Jacobs family has translated pain into action and healing:

> Is this not, rather, the fast that I choose:
> releasing those bound unjustly,
> untying the thongs of the yoke;
> Setting free the oppressed,
> breaking off every yoke?
>
> Is it not sharing your bread with the hungry,
> bringing the afflicted and the homeless into
>   your house;
> Clothing the naked when you see them,
> and not turning your back on your own flesh?
>
> Then your light shall break forth like the dawn,
> and your wound shall quickly be healed;
> Your vindication shall go before you,
> and the glory of the Lord shall be your rear
>   guard.
> Then you shall call,
> and the Lord will answer,
> you shall cry for help, and he will say:
> "Here I am!" (58:6–9).

How many of us become bound by our grief, unable to recover from loss or pain? By claiming God's promise as our own—and Christ's consistent teaching that the greatest mercy and faith would be found among the little, the meek, the humble—we too can rise from our pain and find not only healing but also such beautiful hope. We too can say, "Here I am!"

What began with one tiny baby's all-too-soon passing has become a salve to the brokenhearted on both sides of His Chase. The orphans of Ghana have support, shelter, clothing, and compassion. But perhaps the greater healing has come to the hearts of the Jacobs family, who has seen tiny Baby Chase's spirit reborn in the eyes and smiles of all they serve.

Another person who has sparked some pretty intense rebirths reports for work every day on some of the meanest streets of downtown Los Angeles, in a place through which most people might be afraid to even drive. When he started a simple program called Jobs for a Future out of his Boyle Heights parish in 1984, Gregory Boyle, S.J., was simply looking for some kind of an answer to the horrific gang violence that plagued his parish community. He was burying too many young bodies. It needed to end.

What began in desperation has blossomed into the internationally celebrated nonprofit organization Homeboy Industries. With services that range from tattoo removal to legal, health, and substance-abuse support, the twenty-five-year-old organization has empowered thousands of young men and women to leave behind gang affiliations and begin a new life working together in successful social enterprises.

Listen to Father Greg and you'll hear a heart that is poised to give a full yes despite the risk and pain that accompany all the words and the work. Along with the growth and success he's seen, this man has buried hundreds of the homeboys and homegirls with whom he has served, so he knows the stark pain of loss. But "Father G" persists daily in shining a light for souls that have been given up on, despised, and thought by most to be beyond redemption.

Recently, I tuned in for one of Father G's thought of the day pep talks to a crowd of his "homies" who report to work each day at Homeboy Industries. His words of encouragement to formerly incarcerated young people poured out great hope for kids whom the rest of society has left behind: "Brace yourself, face the fact: You are somebody. You are important. You are worthy. You are wonderful. You are holy, thoroughly good. You are great souls!"

When I read Father Greg's words to myself, I hear the love with which they are delivered. "Brace yourself, Lisa. You are somebody. You are important, Lisa. You are worthy. You are wonderful. You, Lisa, are holy, thoroughly good. You, Lisa, are a great soul!" But I also hear the commission behind the words—the reminder that because I am gifted, I have gifts to give. I have a yes to offer to the world around me, a capacity for generosity of spirit that far exceeds what I believe myself capable of giving. This is likely not a message that the homies have heard too often in their lives before they encountered Father Greg and the family he has built.

Like Jesus Christ, who dined with sinners and refused to cast the first stone, Father Greg and the Homeboy Industries team have recognized that healing comes not through isolation but through community and attachment, and through love. Homeboy Industries is built upon an environment where even the most hopeless can find the ability to give themselves fully to God's will for their lives, and it has prospered because of it. This is a story of the true power of rebirth. Embedded in it is the belief that there is redemption and grace for each of us, even the most broken and lost among us. Because we are somebody—important, worthy, wonderful, thoroughly good, and created so by God—the world is waiting for our yes.

Becoming a Survivor

Part of the intrigue of the place I find myself in at this time in my life is the endless potential for the new, the untested, and the unknown. Clearly, my role as a wife and mother will continue until I draw my last breath. But as my nest empties, that role is changing—evolving into something I don't fully yet recognize.

And so I am pondering. I am playing with the ideas of what my yes to God will look like in the years to come, how I will be called to generously live the rest of my days. Much of that is beyond foretelling, but to control the elements I can, I've created a list of dreams and goals.

Some of these are overtly Christian. I would love to return to school for a graduate degree in theology. I hope to do missionary work in either Latin America or Africa. I would love to see my work on the web blossom into a full-force nonprofit in support of mothers most in need of help.

But there is also an item on my life list that might seem to some to have nothing to do with spirituality: I want to be on *Survivor*. Now, please don't laugh. My desire to participate as a contestant on my favorite television program is probably about as feasible and likely to actually happen as my goal to one day own a red Harley Davidson. But if the thought of me astride a Harley or getting voted off the island at tribal council sends you into fits of laughter, then you mistake my intentions.

Let's set the motorcycle to the side for a moment and focus on what one can possibly gain from being on a reality television show. And keep in mind for a moment that past seasons have indicated that the only chance for taking home the final prize on *Survivor* is to lie, cheat, and sometimes even steal your way to the million dollars. So why do I consider appearing on *Survivor* to be part of my plans for living generously? Since the show is nearing its thirtieth season, I've had some time to think about my motivations. I'd like to see what would happen if I tried to play the game completely above board—working diligently, pushing myself to my physical limits, but also being completely honest about what I would do if I won the prize. Just imagine what good you could do with a million dollars—how many mouths you could feed, schools and homes you could build, bodies and hearts you could heal!

But I'm also honestly very intrigued by the concept of a thirty-nine-day retreat in nature with nothing but the clothes on my back and a community full of people, most of whom would likely not consider the experience even remotely spiritual. I think it would be a fascinating way to ponder the potential God has placed within me and to see how I would react to a life with no material possessions, no earthly distractions, and yes—no coffee and Wi-Fi! While I obviously wouldn't spend the whole thirty-nine days praying, I think it would be an amazing way to commune with the Creator in the majesty of his handiwork and to shine a little bit of joy and light for some of the world to see.

What would happen if you went into *Survivor* letting your competitors know that you had no hidden agendas, only a desire to fully live out the experience, to give 100 percent of yourself emotionally and physically, and potentially to help a few people if by some chance your old-lady-butt wasn't the first to be voted off the island? Jeff Probst and Mark Burnett, if by some odd chance you find this book in your hands, why not make one of my life's goals a reality and find out?!

And why do I share this crazy idea here in a book about being open to God's will for our lives and giving ourselves freely and generously to that will? Along with hoping that my pitch to the *Survivor* execs may actually work, I want to illustrate for you that our yeses have limitless potential, that God's creativity means there is absolutely no reason to box in the possible ways in which we can assent to being God's light in the world around us.

Let's shift the paradigm about exactly what being a generous spirit looks like and where we're called to give. I recently had a Facebook dialogue with a contact who objected to my viewing of a particular movie. As evidence of her rightness, she posted a six-year-old link to a faith-based boycott of the movie's lead actor for another movie he had done. I wished this woman well and explained to her that viewing the movie in question with my sons had motivated a truly brilliant conversation about spirituality, service, and the potential of popular culture to have a positive impact in the world. The movie had really nothing to do with religion, but it was a masterpiece of one character's struggle to live out her yes.

My point here is that I'm personally ready to move beyond comfortable confines to explore the vast potential God is calling me to in my life. When I start to second-guess my worthiness to rise to that call, I remember the followers Jesus called—fishermen, a repentant tax collector, a woman of ill repute. In them, Jesus saw God's grace. He called them, taught them, and challenged them to live up to their full potential, sending them out into the world to shine his light while caring for those in need. They were called to go beyond what they had always known, to leave the comfort of the synagogue with little or no safety net. The disciples' yes was a radical commitment to trust that God had the perfect plan for their lives.

Don't think for a moment that this means I want to leave my church, my home, or my work. They are my bedrock. But it's time to see what tiny seedlings can sprout from that bedrock and where those delicate tendrils may climb, blossom, and reach for the sun. I want to see the supermarket, the airport, the women's shelter, a friend's kitchen—or, yes, even a reality television show—as my mission field. I want to give far more than I take and in the process continually grow, stretch, and challenge my limits. And in doing so, I want to continually (but never obnoxiously) give glory to the One who makes all things possible.

Steps along the Path to Yes

While it's fun to make lists of goals and daydream about all that the future holds, in truth the greatest part of my yes to God takes place within the confines of a very simple existence. I'm continually challenged to remember that "feeding the hungry" often means cooking a square meal in my own kitchen and that "clothing the naked" doesn't mean I can neglect our family's huge laundry pile. Giving myself generously to God's will means loving not only in the ways that feel substantive and important. It also means truly delivering the best effort I have even when my heart is not really into the task at hand.

My sons recently gave me a wonderful gadget that is designed to help me along my path to healthiness. This tiny tracking device slips into a rubber bracelet and, when synchronized with my smartphone, helps me track not only my caloric intake and sleep patterns but every step I take. Since I'm a goal-oriented geek, it's the perfect motivational tool to help me attain my daily goal of walking at least 10,000 steps.

I've been thinking lately about how this small bit of rubber and circuits has made me more active since I began wearing it. Somehow, knowing that I'm only a few hundred steps from my daily benchmark has motivated me on more than one cold night to get out the door for an after-dark jaunt down the cul-de-sac. On one of those brisk walks, I recently pondered why 10,000 steps matters, and why I wouldn't be satisfied with only walking 9,999 steps if I'd given my best effort that day.

In truth, every step I take during the day is a part of my yes to living a healthier lifestyle. The same is true for the steps I take toward my paramount goal in life: an eternity spent in God's loving embrace when my earthly days are done. But just like my daily 10,000 steps, that goal won't be met with a halfhearted effort. Movement, intentional exertion, and a firm daily decision are the only way my generosity of spirit will be authentic.

Truthfully, attaining that full and worthy yes will always be a work in progress. There won't ever be a day in my life when I wake up and think, "Wow, I'm there. I've done it!" So the journey—the steps along the path to heaven—is my daily decision to give my best and to praise God for the grace of his acceptance of my tiny gift.

In 1979, Bishop Ken Untener of Saginaw, Michigan, wrote a prayer for a draft of a sermon to be delivered by his cardinal in memory of departed priests and inspired by the life of the martyred Archbishop Oscar Romero. A staunch defender of the rights of his people and a champion for the poor, Archbishop Romero once penned in his diary the words, "In recent days the Lord has inspired in me a great desire for holiness. I have been thinking of how far a soul can ascend if it lets itself be possessed entirely by God."

As a testament to Archbishop Romero's spirit, Bishop Untener penned what is now called "A Step Along the Way: The Archbishop Oscar Romero Prayer":

> It helps, now and then,
> to step back and take a long view.
> The kingdom is not only beyond our efforts,
> it is even beyond our vision.

We accomplish in our lifetime
only a tiny fraction
of the magnificent
enterprise that is God's work.
Nothing we do is complete,
which is a way of saying
that the kingdom always lies beyond us.
No statement says all that could be said.
No prayer fully expresses our faith.
No confession brings perfection.
No pastoral visit brings wholeness.
No program accomplishes the Church's mission.
No set of goals and objectives includes
everything.
This is what we are about.
We plant the seeds that one day will grow.
We water seeds already planted,
knowing that they hold future promise.
We lay foundations that will need further
development.
We provide yeast that produces far beyond our
capabilities.
We cannot do everything, and there is a sense of
liberation in realizing that.
This enables us to do something, and to do it
very well.
It may be incomplete, but it is a beginning,
a step along the way,
an opportunity
for the Lord's grace to enter and do the rest.

> We may never see the end results, but that is the
> difference between the master
> builder and the worker.
> We are workers, not master builders;
> ministers, not messiahs.
> We are prophets of a future not our own.

Like Archbishop Romero and Bishop Untener, I want to allow myself to be entirely possessed by God. I want each of my days to be filled with forward motion toward the destiny he has in store for me. When my head hits the pillow at the end of each day, I want to be able to express my contrition for the ways I've fallen short of my goals and to give thanks for the forward momentum I've made. I'm happy with being a worker if that role means that I get to lay a few bricks upon the masterpiece God has planned.

There are definitely nights when it seems all I've done is move backward, both spiritually and physically. But I'm actually learning that those steps count as well. They are part of my motion. They make up the entirety of what this journey will hold in store for me. But they best help me when I'm cognizant of what even the backward steps teach me about my path as a whole. I won't ever have a full sense of the total road map of my life. But if I move backward in blindness, I gain nothing but grief. If, on the contrary, my diversion is met with analysis and a desire for understanding, it becomes fuel for the next leg of the voyage.

The Grace of Yes

It's tempting to put our heads down, plow straight ahead, and avoid any potential distractions that keep us from attaining our end goal. Don't they say that a straight line is the shortest distance between two points? How tempted I am on so many days to lock myself in my office, plug away at my work for hours on end with only breaks for prayer and sustenance, and cross all the items off my to-do list!

But when I do this exclusively, my yes is deprived of the fullness of God's grace. Jesus taught us this lesson during his time with us. What an inefficient path God chose to bring us into his plan for salvation! At times, I like to sit and wonder:

> That God sent a tiny baby, delivered through the
>   womb of an unwed mother
> into a world filled with political and religious
>   strife.
> That the baby's birth was met and glorified by
>   shepherds and their flocks,
> and by foreign emissaries who journeyed to him
>   led by the light of a star.
> That his glory was made known by an itinerant
>   preacher clothed in camel's hair.
> That he gathered to himself a ragtag band of
>   followers rather than well-known religious
>   leaders of his time.
> That he paused at every turn to care for the ill,
>   the demon-possessed, and known sinners.

That he knowingly marched toward his condem-
  nation for sins he had not committed.
That he bore the weight of my sins on the cross,
  dying a horrific death so that each of us
  might have life forever.
That he rose from the grave, offering us the
  same promise of an eternity spent forever in
  God's presence.
That he loves me, just as I am.

It's too impractical—too random and ill-conceived to even fully comprehend. And yet our yes to God compels us along this same wild, unpredictable, and unknown trajectory. So I'm desirous of the turns along the path I haven't planned for, the inconvenient pit stops where God invites me to better love him by setting Lisa's plans aside to be his hands and feet here in this place, in his time.

I have no idea where this path will take me in the years ahead. But I want to walk it mindfully, with diligence, exertion, joy, and love. I can't wait to learn, to discover, to mess up, to confess, to have fun, and perhaps even to help a few people along the way.

I can't wait—at path's end and God willing—to fully discover the grace of my yes.

To Ponder

1. Have you experienced moments of rebirth in your life? What did you take from these experiences?

2. When you are witness to friends experiencing the potential of spiritual rebirth, how ready are you to

accompany them along their path? If not very, what can you do to be ready?

3.   Name a few of your life's goals, including the most outlandish, unlikely, or even seemingly laughable.

4.   How do these goals have the potential to lead you closer to God and his will for your life?

5.   If you were to map your steps along your path to God, what would the map look like?

6.   Describe your yes to God as it is now and as you desire it to be.

Let us pray.

Abba, Father, lover of my soul,
I give you myself, my life, and my love
exactly as I am,
and with a vision of all I hope to be
in, with, and through you.
Marred by my human condition and weakness,
I offer you the best of all that you have placed within me
as a sign of my love and endless gratitude.
May I follow the teachings of your son, Jesus.
May I emulate the spotless yes of his mother, Mary.
May I serve as a light of the love you shine upon each of us.
And may my path lead me ever closer to an eternity spent
with you.
I love you, Lord.
I give you my eternal yes.

Amen.

Acknowledgments

In many ways, this book is a departure from my previous work and has been both a tremendously rewarding and greatly challenging project.

For their confidence in this message and their fantastic support throughout the writing process, I thank Tom Grady and my entire team of colleagues at Ave Maria Press. I wish to especially express my endless gratitude to my editor and dear friend Eileen Ponder. Eileen, your yes to and graceful shaping of this work has been nothing short of amazing.

For their daily inspiration and commitment to serving, I thank Sarah Reinhard and our entire team of writers at CatholicMom.com. Your daily sharing of your gifts inspires and educates me profoundly.

To my friends and coworkers in the vineyard at the Patheos Catholic Channel, SQPN, and in the social media and blogosphere worlds, thank you for the many ways in which your profound examples and service have inspired me to be a part of the New Evangelization.

With profound joy, I thank Bishop Armando Ochoa and my pastor, Monsignor Robert Wenzinger for being amazing spiritual shepherds. To Martha Danks Ferguson and my faith family at St. Anthony of Padua, thank you for your continual examples of a worthy yes.

With hugs and smiles to each of my Fresno girlfriends, thank you for gym trips, mahj mornings, breakfast outings, failed knitting lessons, hair appointments, endless cups of coffee, and putting up with all my adventures.

To the Bartholomy and Hendey families, your love inspired so many of the words that fill these pages. Mom and Daddy, you've shown us that faith, family, and lives lived generously are a small glimpse of heaven on earth.

Adam and Eric, your yeses give glory to the God who created you and bring endless joy to your parents. Keep writing the soundtrack of your lives in such fantastic and fun ways.

Greg, you are home. You are my greatest teacher and my very best friend. Here's to our yesses yet to come!

Notes

1. "Matt Maher: Story Behind 'Lord, I Need You,'" New Release Tuesday, published July 31, 2013, http://youtu.be/J59xmqQIpwo.

2. "Pope Francis: Person of the Year," Vatican Radio website, December 11, 2013, http://www.news.va/en/news/pope-francis-person-of-the-year.

3. John de Graaf, David Wann & Thomas H. Naylor, *Affluenza: The All-Consuming Epidemic*, 2nd ed. (San Francisco: Berrett-Koehler Publishers, 2005).

Lisa M. Hendey is the creator of CatholicMom.com and author of *The Handbook for Catholic Moms* and *A Book of Saints for Catholic Moms*. She gives workshops on faith, family, and Catholic new-media topics. Hendey lives with her family in Fresno, California.

AVE

AVE MARIA PRESS

Founded in 1865, Ave Maria Press,
a ministry of the Congregation of
Holy Cross, is a Catholic publishing
company that serves the spiritual and
formative needs of the Church and its
schools, institutions, and ministers;
Christian individuals and families; and
others seeking spiritual nourishment.

For a complete listing of titles from

Ave Maria Press

Sorin Books

Forest of Peace

Christian Classics

visit www.avemariapress.com

AVE MARIA PRESS
Notre Dame, IN
A Ministry of the United States Province of Holy Cross